PROBLEMS OF NEUROSIS

A BOOK OF CASE HISTORIES

hARPER ✦ ᴛoRChbookS

*A reference-list of Harper Torchbooks, classified
by subjects, is printed at the end of this volume.*

RESEARCHES IN THE SOCIAL, CULTURAL AND BEHAVIORAL SCIENCES

EDITED BY
BENJAMIN NELSON

ADLER, ALFRED: Problems of Neurosis: *A Book of Case Histories.* Edited by P. Mairet, Introduction by H. L. Ansbacher. TB/1145

BURRIDGE, KENELM: *Mambu: A Melanesian Millennium.*

CANTRIL, HADLEY: The Invasion from Mars: *A Study in the Psychology of Panic.* New Introduction by the author. TB/1282

DAVIS, ALLISON and DOLLARD, JOHN: Children of Bondage: *The personality development of Negro youth in the Urban South.* TB/3049

DURKHEIM, EMILE, et al.: Essays on Sociology and Philosophy, *with appraisals of Durkheim's life and work.* Edited by Kurt H. Wolff. TB/1151

FESTINGER, LEON, RIECKEN, HENRY W. and SCHACHTER, STANLEY: When Prophecy Fails: *A social and psychological study of a modern group that predicted the destruction of the world.* TB/1132

FINGARETTE, HERBERT: The Self in Transformation: *Psychoanalysis, Philosophy and the Life of the Spirit.* TB/1177

GOULDNER, ALVIN W.: Wildcat Strike: *A Study in Worker-Management Relationships.* TB/1176

GRAÑA, CÉSAR: Modernity and Its Discontents: French Society and the French Man of Letters in the Nineteenth Century. TB/1318

HAMMOND, J. L.: *The Rise of Modern Industry.* Introduction by Max Hartwell

HAMMOND, J. L. and BARBARA: *The Village Labourer.* Introduction by H. J. Habakkuk. *The Skilled Labourer.*

HEGEL, G. W. F.: The Phenomenology of Mind. Introduction by George Lichtheim. TB/1303

LANDY, DAVID: Tropical Childhood: *Cultural Transmission and Learning in a Puerto Rican Village.* TB/1235

LEWIN, KURT: Field Theory in Social Science: *Selected Theoretical Papers,* edited by Dorwin Cartwright. TB/1135

LOCKWOOD, DAVID: *The Black-Coated Worker.* Introduction by Ralf Dahrendorf

MERTON, ROBERT K.; BROOM, LEONARD; COTTRELL, LEONARD S. JR., editors: Sociology Today:

Problems and Prospects, Vol. I, TB/1173; Vol. II, TB/1174

MICHELS, ROBERTO: First Lectures in Political Sociology. Translated with an Introduction by Alfred de Grazia. TB/1224

MOORE, BARRINGTON JR.: Political Power and Social Theory: *Seven Studies.* TB/1221

MOORE, BARRINGTON JR.: Soviet Politics—The Dilemma of Power: *The Role of Ideas in Social Change.* New Introduction by the author. TB/1222

MOORE, BARRINGTON JR.: Terror and Progress—USSR. TB/1266

ROSEN, GEORGE: Madness in Society: *Chapters in the Historical Sociology of Mental Illness.* TB/1337

SAINT-SIMON, HENRI DE: Social Organization, the Science of Man, *and other writings,* edited by Felix Markham. TB/1152

SAMUELSSON, KURT: Religion and Economic Action: *A Critique of Max Weber's* The Protestant Ethic and The Spirit of Capitalism TB/1131

SCHAAR, JOHN H.: Escape from Authority: *The Perspectives of Erich Fromm.* TB/1155

SHERIF, MUZAFER: The Psychology of Social Norms. TB/3072. *Group Relations at the Crossroads.

SIMMEL, GEORG, et al.: Essays on Sociology, Philosophy and Aesthetics, edited by Kurt H. Wolff. TB/1234

THOMAS, W. I.: *The Unadjusted Girl. Introduction by Michael Parenti.

TIRYAKIAN, EDWARD A., editor: Sociological Theory, Values and Sociocultural Change. TB/1316

WARNER, W. LLOYD: A Black Civilization: *A Study of an Australian Tribe.* TB/3056

WARNER, W. LLOYD and ASSOCIATES: Democracy in Jonesville: *A Study in Quality and Inequality.* TB/1129

ZNANIECKI, FLORIAN: *The Social Role of the Man of Knowledge. Introduction by Lewis Coser.

In Preparation

Alfred Adler

PROBLEMS OF NEUROSIS

A BOOK OF CASE HISTORIES

EDITED BY

PHILIP MAIRET

INTRODUCTION TO THE
TORCHBOOK EDITION BY

HEINZ L. ANSBACHER

1964

HARPER TORCHBOOKS
HARPER & ROW, PUBLISHERS
NEW YORK, EVANSTON, AND LONDON

1.75

PROBLEMS OF NEUROSIS

Contents

List of Cases

Introduction to the Torchbook Edition

by Heinz L. Ansbacher

Problems of Neurosis is essentially a collection of cases. To enable the reader for whom this book may represent the first contact with the work of Adler, better to understand this material from the start and to appreciate it in its full significance, we shall attempt in the following to give a frame of reference through an outline of Adler's Individual Psychology. Since, as was his custom, Adler interspersed in the case reports statements touching on nearly every aspect of his theories, it will be possible to support our outline on nearly every point with quotations from the present text.

This introduction will discuss (*a*) the significance of Adler's work, (*b*) his theory of personality, (*c*) his views on mental health, neurosis, and psychotherapy; and give brief accounts of (*d*) his life and (*e*) the present volume.

A. The Significance of Adler's Work

The significance of Adler today is that he was the first to develop a comprehensive theory of personality, psychological disorders and psychotherapy, which represented an alternative to the views of Freud, even long before Freud had reached the climax of his acclaim, and simultaneously with Freud's own later development.

Alternatives to Freud have in recent years been restated by many who found his system inadequate to the problems to which it pertains. These developments are known as existential psychology and psychiatry, client-centered counseling, humanistic psychology, the "third force" in psychology, phenomenological psychology, social psychiatry, rational-emotive psychotherapy, neo-Freudian trends, ego psychology, and by many other names. In the aspects in which they depart from Freud, they all can be reconciled far more easily with the basic assumptions of Adler than with those of Freud. To know Adler is to be well prepared for all these developments.

It seems that in the development of modern psychological thinking the Western world first had to go through the Freudian stage, even as Adler himself did for a short period. Fourteen years younger than Freud, he was from 1902 to 1911 a prominent member of Freud's circle. But then he was the first to free himself from Freud as countless others have done since, although his influence was stimulating and fructifying. Now that one reads with increasing frequency that we have entered the post-Freudian era, the appreciation of and interest in Adler are proportionately growing.

Freud represented a half-way station, so-to-speak. Revolutionary as his theories were and difficult as they seem at first, they were actually more conservative and more easy to understand with reference to the scientific and also to some of the popular thinking then prevailing, than was Adler's thinking. Freud was revolutionary for his day in that he listened to every word of his patients, knowing that this would be valuable basic information for solving the puzzle of mental disorder. But he was scientifically conservative in that he firmly believed that the patient's inner psychological world was ultimately determined by objective causes that rested in his past. Freud was difficult in that he created a large new vocabularly designating numerous drives, stages, areas, and mechanisms which he believed to have "discovered," and which he considered responsible for the full range of human behavior. And yet all this was relatively easy to grasp in that it still was similar to old ways of thinking, according to which mental disorders, like physical illnesses, were caused by forces beyond the individual's control.

It was scientifically more revolutionary to proclaim, as did Adler, that the inner psychological world of the individual, which had such far-reaching consequences, was not objectively caused, but was ultimately the individual's own creation, and that the individual's course of life received its direction not from relatively objective drives, but from his highly subjective goals and values. And it was more difficult to accept that the individual could be quite unaware of the goals and values which he himself had created or accepted, than that he was the pawn of an "unconscious" which supposedly controlled his conscious self.

The essential difference between Freud's and Adler's ways of thinking is that in the former the conception of man's psychological functioning is patterned after the older physical sciences, whereas in the latter it is patterned after the biological sciences, the sciences of life. In the former a mechanistic, elementaristic, and deterministic orientation was adequate. But in the latter it is today widely appreciated that for an understanding of what is specific to life, an organismic and holistic view is more fruitful. Such a view reckons not only with objective determiners from the past, but makes the force of life itself, with its incessant forward urge, the most important determining factor. Although this force is still unexplained and may forever remain so, it is still more scientific to take it importantly into account than to disregard it in the interest of a false scientific ideal. And, as Sinnott[1] has repeatedly explained, it is scientifically fruitful to approach problems of biology from a teleological viewpoint.

If the organismic-holistic viewpoint is the more adequate for biology in general, this must be true especially for the science concerned with the highest manifestation of life, human psychology. Adler embraced this viewpoint, which was not so well defined then as it is today. Its principle practical significance is that the individual is understood not as completely determined by outside forces but to a considerable extent as self-determined. Such a conception is particularly useful in psychotherapy in that it gives the patient a feeling of freedom and optimism, so important in enabling him to change.

B. Theory of Personality

The essential principles of Adler's psychology, which he named Individual Psychology, may be considered to be the following.

1. *Unity of the Individual*

The unit to be studied is the individual person and his way of living. All the general similarities one can observe among people,

---

[1] Sinnott, E. W. *Cell and psyche: the biology of purpose.* Chapel Hill, N. C.: University of North Carolina Press, 1950. New York: Harper Torchbooks, 1961.

such as drives, emotions, cultural experiences, must be understood as subordinated to the individual's organization, his *style of life*, life-plan. As in Gestalt psychology the organization of the whole figure will determine how the parts will be perceived, so in Individual Psychology, the organization of the whole person will influence all his partial functions. But, beyond Gestalt psychology, Adler conceives the individual as goal-oriented, and all partial functions, including neurotic symptoms, as serving the overall purpose.

One of the important consequences of this understanding is that the Freudian conscious-unconscious antithesis and the notion of intrapersonal conflicts are done away with. The unconscious serves the individual's purposes no less than the conscious; it is not a relatively autonomous function which attempts to rule the individual, while he attempts to repress it. "Individual Psychology distinguishes in the conscious and the unconscious, not separate and conflicting entities, but complementary and cooperating parts of one and the same reality" (p. 29). "We cannot oppose 'consciousness' to 'unconsciousness' as if they were two antagonistic halves of an individual's existence. The conscious life becomes unconscious as soon as we fail to understand it—and as soon as we understand an unconscious tendency it has already become conscious" (p. 163).

Not only the psychological but also the organic functions are subordinated to the style of life, although both were originally factors in its formation. "The organic functions are dominated by the style of life. This is notably the case with the lungs, the heart, the stomach, the organs of excretion and the sexual organs. The disturbance of these functions expresses the direction which an individual is taking to attain his goal. I have called these disturbances the organ dialect, or organ jargon, since the organs are revealing in their own most expressive language the intention of the individual totality" (p. 156).

"The dialect of the sexual organs is especially expressive" (p. 156). "My questioners often appear to have been misled . . . into believing that the sexual impulse is the central motive. . . . Our experience is that the sexual components cannot even be correctly estimated except in relation to the individual style of life" (p. 46).

"We are far from disputing that every mental and bodily function is necessarily conditioned by inherited material, but what

TO THE TORCHBOOK EDITION

we see in all psychic activity is the *use which is made* of this material to attain a certain goal" (p. 30).

The individual is not divided against himself. He is not the battleground of conflicting forces. What appears as inner conflicts is derived from man's self-determination, including the freedom and necessity to choose between alternatives presented by the situation. It includes the freedom to make mistakes. "Rightly understood, the whole of this mental process—working from below to above, expressing an inferiority but compensating with a superiority—is not ambivalence but a dynamic unity. Only if it is not understood as a whole do we see it as two contradictory and warring entities" (p. 87).

2. *Unitary Motivation*

As an organism, a unified whole, the individual is not determined by various drives or motives, but there is one dynamic force, of which all others are only partial and subsidiary aspects. This derives from the growth and forward movement of life itself. It is a general forward striving. The recognition of one master motive is common to all organismic psychologies since Adler. Some of the names that have been chosen by recent workers are: self-actualization, self-expansion, self-consistency, competence.

Adler ultimately spoke of striving for perfection, completion, overcoming, or a goal of success. In the present volume he speaks of striving to overcome the difficulties of life (p. 32), the upward strivings of the psyche (p. 33), striving for superiority (p. 13), or, most often, a goal of superiority. Superiority may be personal superiority over others, or superiority over general difficulties, in the sense of perfection, completion, or competence. The former is characteristic of mental disorders, the latter of mental health.

Here a problem arises. Adler's theoretical writing started with the concept of organ inferiority and its compensation, and soon afterwards he stressed feelings of inferiority as a dynamic force. In the present volume we find, "The sense of impotence, or the 'feeling of inferiority,' is the root-conception of Individual Psychology" (p. 33). "We soon perceive a greater or lesser degree of the feeling of inferiority in everyone, together with a compensatory striving towards a goal of superiority" (p. 2).

The problem is: Which comes first, the feeling of inferiority or the striving? A theory of motivation which puts inferiority feelings first would include only what Maslow[2] calls deficit motivation. In this respect compensation is actually a parallel construction to drive-reduction: Without the feeling of a deficit, an inferiority, there would be no striving.

Although Adler never became explicit on this issue, he quietly changed the order in his last writings, putting the striving first. "In comparison with unattainable ideal perfection, the individual is continuously filled by an inferiority feeling and motivated by it." "In the struggle for perfection, man is always in a state of psychical agitation and feels unsettled before the goal of perfection."[3] This is a great improvement of the theory. Not only does it give room for the concept of growth motivation (Maslow), the primacy of the striving also permits one to consider this striving as a human manifestation of the general growth and expansion movement which is characteristic of all of life. Furthermore, it is not possible to verify a universal primary inferiority feeling in the infant. This can be neither observed directly nor ascertained through introspection; it is merely a conjecture, whereas the striving for success or competence can be very readily observed in the infant.[4]

In a paper by Adler[5] published during his last year, summarizing the basic assumptions of Individual Psychology, inferiority feeling is not even mentioned. This does not mean that in the psychology of mental disorders strong inferiority feelings with correspondingly low self-esteem do not remain a central factor. It only means that inferiority feelings are no longer considered primary, but the outgrowth of an impeded striving for success.

[2] Maslow, A. H. "Deficiency motivation and growth motivation" (1955). In *Toward a psychology of being*. Princeton, N. J.: Van Nostrand, 1962. Pp. 19–41.

[3] Adler, A. *The Individual Psychology of Alfred Adler*. New York: Basic Books, 1956. Pp. 23 and 48.

[4] White, R. W. "Adler and the future of ego psychology" (1957). In K. A. Adler & Danica Deutsch (Eds.) *Essays in Individual Psychology*. New York: Grove Press, 1959. Pp. 437–454.

[5] Adler, A. "The progress of mankind" (1937). In K. A. Adler & Danica Deutsch (Eds.) *Essays in Individual Psychology*. New York: Grove Press, 1959. Pp. 3–8.

3. *Self-Determination and Uniqueness*

Since the human individual is capable of considering himself and his situation, and of extending himself into the future, the master motive derives its direction from the over-all goal the individual sets for himself, his conceptualization of superiority or success. Not all of the goal content is conceptualized; to a greater or lesser extent the individual is only dimly aware of where he is heading. To some extent the subject's goal is also the inference or working hypothesis of the psychologist.

While the objective realities have been used in the formulation of the goal, it is in the end subjectively determined by the inventive or creative power of the individual. This is how individual uniqueness becomes most pronounced. Beyond the uniqueness of the constellation of hereditary and environmental factors in each particular case, the goal of superiority which uses these is capable of infinite individual variation.

"No soul develops in freedom. Each one is in mental, emotional and nutritive dependence upon his immediate environment on the earth and in the cosmos, yet so far independent that he must take up these relations consciously: he must answer them as the questions of life" (p. 36). "As a conscious relation between its organism and environment, the child's psyche seems to have an indefinite *causal* power: so that, normal or abnormal, it never reacts with anything like mathematical exactitude. Life, as opposed to dead material, always reacts thus, in a more or less inaccurate—and spontaneous—manner" (p. 34). "The child's individual conception of the future is the dominant causal factor" (p. 90). "In the world of the psyche there is no principle of individual orientation beyond our own beliefs" (p. 62). Our responses to the world will depend on our conception of it, our beliefs and attitudes. Thus Individual Psychology becomes a cognitive and phenomenological psychology.

As already mentioned, what appears as inner conflicts derives from man's freedom to make choices. This freedom offers particular difficulty for the neurotic, because a choice point marks a step forward while the neurotic is afraid of going ahead. Thus where others speak of inner conflicts, Adler speaks of the "hesitating attitude" (p. 3), wasting time (p. 103) in order to gain time.

From the postulate of the importance of beliefs and attitudes in the guidance of behavior and their ultimate determination by the individual's own creative power, follows an optimistic outlook so important for treatment, also mentioned earlier.

4. *The Social Context*

Just as the partial functions cannot be considered out of the context of the individual, so the individual must be considered within his larger context, the human society. An important part of what makes us human, namely language, is a social product, showing how unscientific it would be to study the individual without taking his social context fully into account. Thus Individual Psychology becomes the study of interpersonal transactions.

This is reflected in the following description of the situation developing from a child's feeling dethroned. "It is a common thing for the first child to hasten his own dethronement by fighting against it with envy, jealousy and truculence, which lower him in the parental favour" (p. 102).

Even the function of the sense organs was understood by Adler in the social context. "Imperfections in the sense organs limit the means which a child has of sharing in the life of others" (p. 65).

With regard to the significant problems that man faces, they are all of a social nature. "We must realize that every adaptation we have to make in life, from kindergarten to business management, from school chums to marriage, is, directly or indirectly, a social action. From the earliest times, we face new thoughts and events in a manner which is dominantly social or antisocial, it cannot be neutral. Suppose, for instance, that a boy is terrified by illness and death in his environment. He may allay his fears by the determination to be a doctor, and to fight against death. This is obviously a more social idea than that of being a grave-digger, the one who buries the *others*—a reaction which I have also found in a boy in that situation" (p. 33).

5. *Social Interest*

In the organismic-holistic view, man is not seen in unavoidable conflict with society and its rules. This does not deny the existence of such conflicts, but does deny their unavoidability. The concept of society itself is only an abstraction. In concrete reality there are only individuals and rules that they have made to facilitate the process of living together. Everyone has the capacity of understanding these "rules of the game," of developing them further, and of contributing something which will become a part of "society" which another individual may have to meet. Human nature "includes the possibility of socially affirmative action" (p. 35).

"The high degree of cooperation and social culture which man needs for his very existence demands spontaneous social effort, and the dominant purpose of education is to evoke it. Social feeling is not inborn; but it is an innate potentiality which has to be consciously developed" (p. 31). The German term is *Gemeinschaftsgefühl*, which has also been translated as social interest. It is not an innate altruistic motive, opposed to a selfish motive. This would be a motivational dualism, foreign to a holistic theory. Social interest is rather a cognitive function which must be *consciously* developed through education. It may, however, acquire secondary motivational attributes like any developed capacity such as typing or skiing. Man likes to do what he is capable of doing well.

The concept of social feeling or social interest is today recognized as one of Adler's extremely important contributions. It is particularly important for a definition of positive mental health which offers such great difficulty to other theories which do not have this concept.

C. Theory of Mental Health, Neurosis, and Psychotherapy

1. *Mental Health*

While the definition of positive mental health is still an extensively discussed problem, Adler clearly recognized the necessity of formulating a widely serviceable answer. He generally did not describe mental disturbances as "illness" but showed how they were mistaken ways of living, mistaken life styles. He designated those with mistaken life styles as "failures." Thus mental health could never be the mere absence of illness, but was a less faulty way of living. The aim of his therapeutic efforts was "to replace the great mistakes by small ones. . . . Big mistakes can produce neuroses, but little mistakes a nearly normal person" (p. 62).

Adler phrased his therapeutic aim in this modest fashion because he had no absolute answer to the right way of living. We still do not have the answer and probably never shall have, as we have no absolute answer to the meaning of life.

In the face of this dilemma, presented by the necessity of a definition of the right way of living on the one hand, and the impossibility of giving an absolute answer, Adler resorted to a pragmatic answer. Adler observed that those who could be called mentally healthy led lives which in the long run were socially more useful in a broad sense than the lives led by those who could be called mentally "sick." Consequently he made social usefulness the criterion of mental health.

"By useful I mean in the interests of mankind generally. The most sensible estimate of the value of any activity is its helpfulness to all mankind, present and future, a criterion that applies not only to that which subserves the immediate preservation of life, but also to higher activities such as religion, science, and art" (p. 78). The healthfulness of such striving is determined by the order of the world according to which a self-centered goal is bound to be limited and precarious, whereas a self-transcending useful goal has the greatest validity attainable.

Such usefulness is the outcome of a well developed social feeling or social interest. "It is almost impossible to exaggerate the value of an increase in social feeling. The mind improves, for intelligence is a communal function. The feeling of worth and value is heightened, giving courage and an optimistic view, and there is a sense of acquiescence in the common advantages and drawbacks of our lot. The individual feels at home in life and feels his existence to be worthwhile just so far as he is useful to others and is overcoming common instead of private feelings of inferiority. Not only the ethical nature, but the right attitude in aesthetics, the best understanding of the beautiful and the ugly will always be founded upon the truest social feeling" (p. 79).

A similar passage reads: "Courage, an optimistic attitude, common sense, and the feeling of being at home upon the crust of the earth, will enable him to face advantages and disadvantages with equal firmness. His goal of superiority will be identified with ideas of serving the human race and of overcoming its difficulties by his creative power" (pp. 47–48). Here Adler characterizes the way of life of the individual "who has been well prepared for social life" (p. 47) through development of his social interest. Such a person will also "solve all love-problems with loyalty to the partner and responsibility to society" (p. 47).

2. The Neurotic Style of Life

By contrast, the neurotic life style is essentially that of the pampered child. Such a person does not contribute, but rather leans on others and is likely not to take responsibility for his actions but to shift responsibility and blame upon other factors or other people.

"In the investigation of a neurotic style of life we must always suspect an opponent, and note who suffers most because of the patient's condition. Usually this is a member of the family, and sometimes a person of the other sex, though there are cases in which the illness is an attack upon society as a whole. There is always this element of concealed accusation in neurosis, the patient feeling as though he were deprived of his *right*—i.e., of the center of attention—and wanting to fix the responsibility and blame upon someone. By such hidden vengeance and accusation, by excluding social activity whilst fighting against persons and rules, the problem-child and the neurotic find some relief from their dissatisfaction" (p. 81).

The dissatisfaction stems from the fact that such a person is not prepared when he comes to face the general life problems of society, work, and love, all of which require cooperation and social interest for their satisfactory solution. "All neurotic persons who have developed from a pampered prototype expect to be appreciated *before* they will do anything of social value instead of *after* having done it, thus expecting the natural course of things to be reversed in their own favor" (p. 77). Such people want "to take without giving" (p. 95) want "everything for nothing" (p. 94) and "all or nothing" (p. 55). The result often is nothing.

When an impasse is reached, the neurosis breaks out into the open. The patient shows disabling symptoms. These serve to safeguard his self-esteem and to provide excuses for his failure before himself and others. At the same time the symptoms are hidden accusations of others whom he considers not to have done enough for him. "Neurosis invariably gives relief to the subject, not, of course, in the light of objectivity and common sense, but according to his own private logic: it secures some triumph or at least it allays the fear of defeat. Thus neurosis is the weapon of the coward, and the weapon most used by the weak" (p. 80). "The problem of every neurosis is, for the patient, the difficult maintenance of a style of acting, thinking and perceiving which distorts and denies the demands of reality" (p. 1).

This description of the neurotic may seem harsh. But Adler also makes the important categorical statement: "Every neurotic is partly in the right" (p. 24). By this is meant that he has "good" reasons for his behavior—only, they are not sufficient reasons. The neurotic generally suffered from organ inferiorities or was pampered or neglected as a child (pp. 34–37), all three situations being conducive to the development of the pampered, non-contributive style of life, as Adler formulated it in a later publication. "In these three types of children we encounter the three typical accentuations of the feeling of inferiority. They all weaken the social contact, and tend to isolate the individual in an ever-narrowing sphere of interest" (p. 37).

The point is that the individual was misled by such situations toward his mistaken style of life. To understand a case means to arrive at the conclusion: Considering the circumstances of the patient and his original mistaken interpretation, he is acting quite logically, and we would respond the same way, given the same premises. Thus we can empathize and sympathize with the neurotic, and also remain hopeful regarding the possibility of change.

3. *Psychotherapy*

If mental health is striving for a goal of superiority or success which is one of general benefit, and if mental disorder is a mistaken striving for a goal which has no general validity, one of personal superiority, then the task of psychotherapy becomes a re-orientation of the patient toward a more useful objective for his striving. The patient came to the therapist because he reached an impasse with regard to a specific life situation with which he is presently confronted. "We must make a change in the deeper motive, in the underlying style of life, and then the patient will see all his life-tasks in a new perspective" (p. 19). The outcome is a cognitive reorganization.

The mistaken goal stems, as we have seen, from an underdeveloped social interest and increased inferiority feelings. It thus becomes the task of the therapist to encourage the patient and to strengthen his social interest. This is done by the therapist himself first extending a sincere social interest to the patient. Thus psychotherapy is at once repudiated as a detached technology, and becomes a sincere interpersonal relationship.

"The patient must be appealed to in a friendly way, coaxed into a receptive frame of mind. Indeed, the task of the physician or psychologist is to give the patient the experience of contact with a fellow-man, and then to enable him to transfer this awakened social feeling to others. This method, of winning the patient's good will, and then transferring it to his environment, is strictly analogous to the maternal function. The social duty of mother-hood is to interpret society to the individual, and if the mother fails in this, the duty is likely to devolve much later upon the physician who is heavily handicapped for the task. The mother has the enormous advantage of the physical and psychic relation; she is the greatest experience of love and fellowship that the child will ever have. . . . This is the two-fold function of motherhood, to give the child the completest possible experience of human fellowship, and then to widen it into a life-attitude towards others" (pp. 20–21).

"What the Freudians call transference (so far as we can discuss it apart from sexual implication) is merely social feeling" (p. 73). "We are far from denying that other schools of psychiatry have their successes in dealing with neuroses, but in our experience they do so less by their methods than when they happen to give the patient a good human relation with the physician, or above all, to give him encouragement" (p. 40).

The task of the therapist is to enable the patient "to realize what he is doing, and to transfer his egocentric interest to social life and useful activity" (p. 40). The cure depends on the patient's understanding his self-centered goal "which has been hitherto a heavily-guarded secret" (pp. 73–74) from his own understanding.

But Adler made the cure not dependent on such insight alone. He also had a place for therapy without insight, such as milieu therapy, or as we often say today, social therapy. "It is true, that, in lighter cases, a patient with very varied symptoms may lose them before he himself or the doctor have come to grasp their coherence. When this happens it is either because of a favorable change in the patient's situation or because the doctor, by encouragement or by chance, renews the patient's interest in others" (p. 54).

D. About Adler

Alfred Adler was born on February 7, 1870 in Vienna, where he lived most of his life. Even as a young physician he applied his medical knowledge to social and educational problems. In 1902 he was, with three others, invited by Freud for discussions at the latter's residence. This group was the beginning of the Vienna Psychoanalytic Society. In 1910 Adler became its president and co-editor of one of its journals. By 1911 he and Freud felt that their views could no longer be reconciled, and Adler founded his own school and journal of Individual Psychology. His society eventually expanded to 34 local units all over Europe, especially Germany.

Since Adler keenly felt the necessity for practical application of psychological insights, he lectured widely and established the first child guidance clinics in Vienna. From 1926 on he visited the United States regularly and settled in New York in 1935. He died suddenly while on a lecture tour in Scotland, on May 28, 1937. At the time of his death he held the chair of medical psychology at the Long Island Medical College, now the State University of New York, Downstate Medical Center.

Informal discourse and lectures were Adler's favored means of communication. He held these not only for professional audiences and students, but also for laymen. While he wrote well over a hundred major articles, most of these were based on lecture notes, as were most of his books.

He was a most democratic, friendly, hospitable person with a love for informal sociability, music, and all the arts, including gardening. He was married and the father of four children, two of whom are carrying on his work, practicing psychiatry in New York today. They are Dr. Alexandra Adler and Dr. Kurt A. Adler.

A man of great energy, he combined his enjoyment of life with an equally marked capacity for work. Philip Mairet, the editor of *Problems of Neurosis*, who knew him well, evaluates him as follows: "Adler was, as I and others who met him felt, a great man. He had not the vast breadth and depth of culture of Freud or of Jung; but he knew enough in that respect for his purpose, and what he knew he knew very well. First and foremost, he knew human nature very deeply. More directly than the other great psychotherapists, he was a moralist, but there was no moralic acid in him. He came to psychology as a practical physician, who wanted to cure people's disabilities or help them to compensate for them if they were partly incurable. I believe his diagnostic eye was practically keener than Freud's or Jung's, who were greater men in some other respects, and great writers which Adler was not. Adler was wonderfully spontaneous, and most of his best lecturing was delivered impromptu." [6]

E. About the Present Volume

1. *History*

The present volume is taken from lectures Adler had given in English. In 1928 Mairet was handed a sheaf of notes and reports of these lectures with the view of editing them into a book. Mairet was well qualified to do this. He was a journalist interested in philosophy and psychology who subsequently became editor of the *New English Weekly,* a review of public affairs, literature, and the arts, who translated and edited numerous books. He had attended many of Adler's London lectures and had already published a small volume of his own on Adler's psychology.[7]

Mairet writes about these notes and reports: "Some of these were Adler's own notes from which he spoke; others were, as I remember, reports stenographed or written up by enthusiasts who heard the lectures. Whether Adler had already been lecturing in the U.S.A. at that time I do not remember. I fancy he had been there once.[8] It is possible that the lectures had all been given in London, to medical and psychological societies. Anyhow, they were all in English, which Adler spoke fluently enough, but not an English one could well print. I undertook to make these lectures into the book which was published as *Problems of Neurosis.*

"I discharged my editorial duty, which was really that of re-writing the whole of the material entrusted to me, very much to

[6] Personal communication, January 13, 1963.

[7] Mairet, P. *ABC of Adler's psychology.* London: Kegan Paul, 1928.

[8] Adler made the first of his regular tours to the United States during the winter 1926–1927.

Adler's satisfaction. Half-way through the work, he saw what I had done so far, and wrote to me saying: 'Do not fear to elaborate or extend *in our sense.*' I felt flattered at this, but did not, to any great degree, if at all, avail myself of the permission to 'gloss' his argument, although I often had to interpret meagre notes at considerable length. I do not remember that he made any corrections to my final manuscript." [9]

The lack of systematization of the notes from which Mairet started was still reflected in the original edition by the absence of chapter titles. Instead, the chapters were preceded by some twelve more or less unconnected subheadings on the average. These have now been replaced by single titles so chosen that they would illuminate what in our opinion is most specific to each chapter. But it must be understood that none of the chapters is "pure" in the sense of dealing exclusively with what its title indicates; rather, there is a good deal of overlapping between chapters.

In addition, all cases of at least one page in length, thirty-seven in all, have been marked off and given titles to facilitate their identification, in the hope thereby to increase the usefulness of this volume.

Three chapters have been reprinted previously, at various occasions and under various titles. They are Chapter VI, "Neurotic Use of Emotions;"[10] Chapter VII, "The Family Constellation;"[11] and Chapter VIII, "Early Recollections," which has been reprinted twice.[12] These last two chapters present Adler's most important methodological contributions to personality appraisal, both of which have attained considerable prominence in recent years. Adler's third specific contribution to personality appraisal, his theory of dream interpretation, is stated in the present volume only briefly, in Chapter X.

[9] Personal communication, January 13, 1963.

[10] Reprinted under the title "The Drive for Superiority." in H. Greenwald (Ed.) *Great cases in psychoanalysis,* New York: Ballantine Books, 1959, pp. 175–186.

[11] Reprinted under the title "Position in family constellation influences life-style," *Int. J. Indiv. Psychol.,* 1937, 3, pp. 211–227.

[12] Reprinted under the title "Significance of early recollections," *Int. J. Indiv. Psychol.,* 1937, 3, pp. 283–287, and in E. L. Hartley, H. G. Birch, and Ruth E. Hartley (Eds.) *Outside readings in psychology,* New York: Crowell, 1950, pp. 361–365.

2. *Contemporary Significance*

The most striking characteristic of the cases presented here is that they are in plain language. They may also seem trivial. There are no dramatic heroes who have become victims of their fate with its dark intricacies, although Adler shows that the neurotic likes to consider himself a tragic hero (pp. 79 and 84). The cases of other psychologists may offer more dramatic reading exactly because, like the layman and the patient, they assume unconscious, uncanny and mysterious internal forces of which the patient has become the hapless victim. The condition for a drama, the presence of a protagonist and his antagonists, is met in the assumption of conflicting forces all within one person.

This dramatic quality is absent when you assume the unity of the individual and his orientation towards a self-created goal. Then you can develop a case history only by showing the mistake in his way of life which the patient himself made, although he had not been aware of his mistake. This may add tragedy but not drama. Furthermore, it is the nature of the mistake itself which makes for triviality, because it is found in the self-centered socially useless character of the goal.

If this kind of approach is as successful as the more dramatic approach, and there is no evidence to the contrary, it is to be given preference. According to the principle of parsimony, if two theories accomplish the same, the simpler of the two is preferable because it lends itself more readily to verification.

A general difficulty encountered with students is that they are replete with the professional jargon of the day and proceed to clothe cases of their own in these terms. While they thus obscure the uniqueness of the case in its concrete life situation, they derive the satisfaction of "verifying" the drives, needs, mechanisms, developmental stages, etc. which they believe compose the individual, and of sounding "professional." They do not appreciate that these are only constructions, abstractions, not life realities; that at their best they are only devices for helping the individual with his problems; and that at their worst, taken for realities, they may pronounce the hopelessness of the case. Students do not sufficiently appreciate that the best case study is one which develops a self-consistent model of a unique individual which would afford an understanding of his unique circumstances and the uniqueness in which he in particular went astray—in order that the individual may then take an alternative approach to the solution of his problems.

Adler was master in achieving such directly pertinent simplicity in interpreting a case to himself and the patient. Technically this would be called the idiographic, phenomenological and natural-history approach, enriched by the relatively few basic assumptions of Adler's theory.

With these considerations in mind, we believe, the present case material and the theory from which it emerged could become particularly useful in the general training of students of clinical psychology, guidance, psychotherapy, social work and all areas concerned with understanding and helping individuals.

University of Vermont
Burlington, Vermont
May 1, 1964

This introduction was prepared in collaboration with my wife, Rowena R. Ansbacher. Her unfailing and indispensable help here, as in all my work, is most gladly and gratefully acknowledged.

H.L.A.

I

Useless Goals of Superiority

THE problem of every neurosis is, for the patient, the difficult maintenance of a style of acting, thinking and perceiving which distorts and denies the demands of reality. Usually, it is not until this way of life has become difficult to the verge of breakdown that the case is brought to the physician, whose task is to find the right method for its correction. The common problem, therefore, of both patient and physician, and the basis of their co-operation, is to understand the nature of the patient's mistakes, and this demands not only a true outline of his essential history, but a perception of the dynamic unity of that history as a continual tension towards an implied conception of superiority.

As the work of Individual Psychologists has abundantly proved, an individual goal of superiority is the determining factor in every neurosis, but the goal itself always originates in—and is strictly conditioned by—the actual experiences of *inferiority*. The physician's first line of approach is to identify the real causes of the feelings of inferiority, which the patient disguises from himself in various degrees and in his individual manner. Since the feeling of inferiority is generally regarded as a sign of weakness and as something shameful, there is naturally a strong tendency to conceal it. Indeed, the effort of concealment may be so great that the person himself ceases to be aware of his inferiority as such, being wholly preoccupied with the consequences of the feeling and with all the objective details that subserve its concealment. So efficiently may an individual train his whole mentality for this task that the entire current of his psychic life flowing ceaselessly from below to above—that is, from the feeling of inferiority to that of superiority—occurs automatically and escapes his own notice.

It is not surprising, therefore, that we often receive a negative reply when we ask a person whether he has a feeling of inferiority. It is better not to press the point, but to observe his mental and psychic movements, in which the attitude and individual aim can always be discerned. In this way we soon perceive a greater or lesser degree of the feeling of inferiority in everyone, together with a compensatory striving towards a goal of superiority. Such a universal feeling is not in itself indictable : its meaning and value depend entirely upon how it is used. The most important discovery of Individual Psychology is that it may be used as a stimulus to continue upon the useful side of life.

A BOY AFRAID OF MAKING DECISIONS

These general observations apply closely to the case of a seventeen-year-old boy, the second child in the family, who was brought to me because he suffered from anxiety, and became extremely angry when confronted with difficulties. He also had stomach trouble and diarrhœa when he went mountaineering, a sport which he sometimes shared with his comrades. His mother was intelligent, and liked him, but apparently preferred his elder brother who gave her less trouble. This elder brother was much stronger, taller and a good sportsman. The father was a capable man, and the patient esteemed him highly.

This boy was afraid of making any decisions because his feeling of inferiority was too great for him to trust himself. He was unwilling, however, to admit that this feeling was due to any cause within his control. He insisted that he was born such as he was, and his nature was no responsibility of his.

This patient's attitude to life was one of hesitation. When confronted with problems he always made difficulties, but though he thus " slowed down " he did not stop altogether. He was a very good pupil at school, but in constant fear of losing even this advantage, and he could not decide at all what to do upon leaving the High School. He made no friends ; did not like girls, and was afraid of sexual experiences. He believed some of his difficulties to be the result of masturbation and pollutions. All this shows typical indecision and lack of confidence in regard to the three problems of life—society, occupation, and love. To all three questions the answer was evaded or postponed. He disguised his sense of general inadequacy by making various *causes* responsible, and thus he reassured and convinced himself of worth. It is notable, however, that the patient went on in spite of difficulties. He studied well, and he climbed mountains—which latter activity, by the way, is a common device of persons who feel themselves overburdened with life, to give themselves feelings of superiority.   To review and emphasise the difficulties of life from the vantage-ground of a superior feeling is the next best thing to being able to boast that one has overcome them.   It was in order to escape from the consciousness of his inferiority-feeling that this patient blamed his weakness upon natural difficulties and masturbation, and especially upon inherited deficiencies.

The theory of heredity must never be emphasised in education or in the theory and practice of psychology.   Except in cases of sub-normal children and congenital idiots it is proper to assume that everyone can do everything necessary.   This is not, of course, to deny the differences of inherited material, but what is important is always the use which is made of it.   In this way only do we see the enormous significance of education.   Right education is the method of developing the individual, with all his inherited abilities and disabilities.   By courage and training disabilities may be so compensated that they even become great abilities.   When correctly encountered, a disability becomes the stimulus that impels towards a higher achievement.   We are no longer surprised to find that those who have attained remarkable successes in life have often been handicapped in the beginning with disabilities and with great feelings of inferiority.   On the other hand, we find that a person who believes himself to be the victim of inherited deficiencies and disabilities, lessens his efforts with a feeling of hopelessness, and his development is thus permanently retarded.

Teachers exaggerate the maleficence of hereditary factors to excuse the inefficiency of their own methods.   It is interesting to read in Einhardt's biography of Charlemagne that this great Emperor could learn neither reading nor writing, from sheer lack of talent for such things ! Now, with the development of educational method, no normal child finds these tasks beyond it. From this and many another example it appears that whenever authors, teachers or parents fail to find a method to correct errors by education they blame the inherited deficiencies. The superstition which this habit engenders is one of the greatest difficulties and the most commonly encountered in education and in handling " problem children," not to mention the treatment of criminals, neurotics and psychotics. Yet for the treatment of these conditions the only reasonable assumption is that which is made by Individual Psychology—that everyone is equal to his life-task. This does not mean that the results are or can be equal, for, of course, inequalities of training, method, and above all the degree of courage shown must be taken into consideration.

To return to the case in question : the ability of this boy's father was an additional reason for his feeling that he could not make good in life. It is well known that the children of great men are very often unsuccessful : they feel incapable of ever attaining positions as high as their fathers held, and therefore do not seriously attempt anything at all. In the case of this patient, the high achievements of his elder brother also lengthened his distance from the goal of superiority in the family circle. He felt himself hopelessly surpassed. The neurosis which he developed was a protection from the painful consciousness of this inferiority. It was the adoption of an attitude which signified to him :— " If I were not anxious, if I were not ill, I should be able to do as well as the others. If my life were not full of terrible difficulties, I should be the first." By this attitude a person is able still to feel superior, for the decision of his worth and value is placed beyond proof, in the realm of possibilities. His chief occupation in life is to look for difficulties, to find means of increasing them, or at least of increasing his own sense of their gravity. The most ordinary difficulties of life, common to everybody, are carefully collected by him and kept upon exhibition. He does this more to impress himself than others, but naturally other people take his burdens into account and do not expect so much of him. Any success he may have, moreover, is magnified by this heavily-advertised handicap, so that it becomes his most useful possession. By it he wins his way to a privileged life, judged by a more lenient standard than others. At the same time, he pays the costs of it with his neurosis.

AGORAPHOBIA WITH HEART SYMPTOMS

Another case of anxiety neurosis, taking the form of agoraphobia, and accompanied by heart symptoms, occurred in a man of thirty-five. Anxiety neurosis is always symptomatic of a timid attitude towards the three problems of life, and those who suffer from it are invariably " spoiled " children.

This man dreamt, " I crossed the limit of the border between Austria and Hungary, and they wanted to imprison me." (Such short dreams, by the way, are the best for analysis.) This dream indicated the man's desire to come to a standstill, due to the fear that he would be defeated if he went on. Its interpretation very well confirms our understanding of anxiety neuroses. The man wanted to limit the scope of his activity in life, to " mark time " so as to gain time. He came to see me because he wished to marry, and the imminent prospect of doing so had brought him to a halt. This fact itself, that he came to consult me about his marriage, clearly indicated his attitude towards it. Similarly, the way that he would behave in marriage was mirrored in the dream, in which he commanded himself—" Do not pass the limit ! " The prison in the dream also reflected the dreamer's view of marriage. We often deceive ourselves by such images in dreams. We use them to train ourselves to tackle the problems of the near future in a manner consistent with our own *style of life*—but not in accordance with the logic of the situation.

— — — — — —

The style of life is founded in the first four or five years of childhood. This period closes with the full development of the ego and the consequent fixation of its attitude to life. From this time onward the answers to the questions put by life are dictated, not by the truth of relations in themselves, but by certain automatised attitudes, which we call the *style* of the individual. Thus we explain the fact that a certain mistake of adaptation—such as the desire to be the centre, to be overburdened, not to be forced, not to be curtailed, etc.—may persistently continue throughout a life-time.

FEAR OF HIGH BUILDINGS

A very successful man, forty years old, complained that he could not go up into a high building without having an impulse to jump out of a window. He said he had always been afraid of everything. He had been the youngest of six children, and very much spoiled by his mother. This case reveals at a glance the wish to be thought over-burdened and in danger. The patient cannot avoid going upstairs, but he colours this procedure with his desire to be in a dangerous situation, clinching the danger by developing an impulse to jump.

In this case and the two previously cited, the goal of superiority is similar, as regards the motive of being overburdened. But this man goes further. He has a desire to jump from a window, but lo ! he overcomes it and still lives. He is stronger even than himself.

In support of this diagnosis I will add a recollection from the patient's childhood. " I went to school when I was six years old. I was not very happy. The very first day a boy attacked me. I was dreadfully afraid and trembled but . . . I sprang at him and threw him down." This fragment of memory records the two typical motives of the man's life-style. He trembles at first, but only to overcome. And that little word " but " holds the rich meaning of his compensation for feelings of inferiority.

A GIRL SUFFERING FROM OBSESSIONS

A girl of twenty-seven came to consult me after five years of suffering. She said : " I have seen so many doctors that you are my last hope in life." " No," I answered, " not the last hope. Perhaps the last but one. There may be others who can help you too." Her words were a challenge to me ; she was *daring* me not to cure her, so as to make me feel bound in duty to do so. This is the type of patient who wishes to shift responsibility upon others, a common development of spoiled children. It is safe to assume that in childhood she constantly contrived to keep another person occupied with her ; and we may infer that it was probably her mother. We need additional facts to verify this impression, but there are methods by which it can be done even in the first interview.

It is important, by the way, to evade such a challenge as the one I have recorded here. The patient may have worked up a high tension of feeling about the idea that the doctor is his " last hope," but we must accept no such distinction. To do so would prepare the way for grave disappointment, or even suicide.

This girl was a second child, whose elder sister was more beautiful than herself, besides being very clever and popular ; so that the patient's life had been like a breathless race to overtake her rival. The sister married happily. The patient also developed well, especially intellectually, outdoing her elder sister in school work. However, the sister was much more charming and attractive, and made friends far more readily. The life of the older sister had been smoother and pleasanter, giving her greater self-confidence. The younger, from a sense of insecurity, felt a need to assert herself against others, which repulsed their friendship. Doubtless none of these two girls' acquaintances recognised the true nature and origin of this difference between them ; but they all felt it unconsciously, and they were attracted to the one and repelled by the other.

The patient had been in love at the age of fourteen, when she was ridiculed for it, so she had ever since declined to play the part of a loving woman. When her sister married she fell in love with a married man. Such an attachment cannot, in itself, be dogmatically estimated. Nobody can be sure if such a love will turn out well or not. But we cannot ignore the fact that every girl in such a situation sees the great difficulties it involves quite as clearly as her parents or anybody else can see them. And a girl going through such an experience tells herself " This is what love is like." Her selection of such a troublesome love is *prima facie* ground for suspicion that she does not wish to see love and marriage through. In this case we see the patient adopted, towards this new life-problem of love, the same hesitant, non-committal attitude she had exhibited in the past. There were reasons. She was less attractive than her sister, and she had been ridiculed in her first love-affair. A girl of such a competitive nature, bent towards the goal of superiority, is always in danger of losing courage and self-confidence by marriage. She will usually feel marriage to be a menace to her sense of superiority. The happy marriage of this girl's sister fed these fears : so did the unhappy marriage of her parents and her mother's inferiority.

The girl's hesitating attitude to love and marriage came out during frank discussion with her. She said : " I am sure my husband would leave me two weeks after our marriage." When I hinted at the deep feeling of inferiority which was the cause of her evasion of marriage she tried to retract this statement : but the mere fact that such an idea could appear at all, even in a joke, showed that her mind had been occupied with that specific problem.

Even when the man with whom she was in love wanted to kiss her she ran away from his caresses. In such ways she established her distance from the demands of love and marriage, and sacrificed everything to her neurotic goal of superiority. " *If* this man were not married I would marry him " was her answer to this problem of life.

" If " is usually the *leit-motif* of the neurotic drama. " If " is the last resort in every neurotic dilemma, and the one sure way of escape. For the *will to escape* there is only one reason, and that is fear of defeat, which is the hardest of all reasons to admit. At this point, therefore, we frequently find some fictitious form of anxiety, which the patient interprets to himself variously but never truly—never, that is, as the simple fear of being beaten. Agoraphobia, anxiety neurosis, and all the forms of phobia may originate at this point, but, whichever it may be, it fulfils its purpose of blocking the way to further activity. Thus what was desired is attained—namely, the ordeal is evaded without disclosing, even to its owner, the hated feeling of inferiority. All the other neurotic symptoms, such as compulsion ideas, fits, fatigue, sleeplessness, functional disturbances such as neurotic heart, headaches, migraine and so on, develop out of the severe tension of this very difficult concealment.

The organs most disturbed by this tension are those which have been made susceptible by some inherited weakness. Hence, we find, where a whole family is liable to a particular organic weakness, that several members suffer from organic illnesses, and others from neurotic symptoms of that same organ. In such cases we must not overlook the contributory factor of imitation. We find, however, in distinction from other psychologists, that the only symptoms imitated are those which are alignable to the neurotic goal of superiority.

This patient had held a position in an office, where she played a leading rôle and was much appreciated, but, like all people with an excessive feeling of inferiority, she was insatiable of appreciation, and always striving for more. At the age of nineteen she changed her position, and lost the admiration she had formerly enjoyed. Reviewing her case, we may note—

1. She was hopeless of competing with her sister, either in making friends or in making a successful marriage.

2. She feared to face the problems of love and marriage.

3. She had lost a favourable position in her work.

In short, all the defeats she had feared had now befallen her; her intense feeling of inferiority had been justified. She did not reason out the situation in this way, but showed, by the appropriate mood, that this was how she felt it.

We may note in passing a typical concentration upon, and exaggeration of, one point in the life-problem, namely, the fear of defeat. While occupied upon the useful side of life one has always to reckon with possibilities of defeat, which we normally minimise by regarding occasional reverses as incidental to every human enterprise. But in such a case as we are now reviewing, the possibility of defeat has become the focus of life. The patient subordinates his whole life to it, just as a person with a cleaning mania makes her life revolve around the idea of dirt and the normal and useful act of washing becomes exaggerated into a ceaseless search for dirt, either upon her own person or upon furniture, floors or elsewhere, until it has no meaning or value for life. Such a mistaken focus of attention is typical of neurosis in general, and in the case of this girl her earlier life-purpose on the useless side—to surpass her sister—was developing into the still narrower and more negative aim of escaping from any sort of defeat whatever.

It is at such a critical point in a life-history that neurotic symptoms are developed. There is no change in the style of life with its characteristic halt at every possibility of defeat : but the individual now fixes this attitude of stoppage, by demanding impossible securities. If he has no means of proving superiority on the useful side he becomes a problem child, or a criminal, or he may commit suicide. If he has some activity, but an insufficient one, and more hope, he deceives himself that he is blocked by a fatal hindrance, such as an illness. He selects certain symptoms and develops them until they impress him as real obstacles. His state of tension readily provides the initial mental or bodily disturbances, which are of various kinds according to the style of life and the native organic weaknesses. Behind his barricade of symptoms the patient feels hidden and secure. To the question, " What use are you making of your talents ? " he answers, " This thing stops me ; I cannot go ahead," and points to his self-erected barricade. We must never neglect the patient's own use of his symptoms. Not only does he use them in this way, but—as happens still more in psychosis—they also modify his perception of every vital question of life.

To be already overworked by grappling with his own neurotic difficulties is not only an extenuating circumstance, it is also a patient's inner relief from his striving for superiority—he really expects less of himself. Such a self-protective style of life may also take the form of being overwhelmed with social difficulties.

The best way to understand a neurotic patient is to set aside all his neurotic symptoms, and to study his style of life and his individual goal of superiority. Only by a firm grasp of these two things can we come to a full understanding of the neurosis itself, the development of which they entirely control. It is the fear of a defeat, real or imaginary, which occasions the outbreak of the so-called neurotic symptoms. Life and custom drag the man along in apparent agreement, but in reality a sense of utter abasement has divided him from life, and he is trying to stop or escape. My experience proves that psychoses such as schizophrenia, mania, melancholia, and paranoia, appear when the patient feels absolutely checkmated, with no hope of going on— which means that he gives up all attempts to answer the three questions of life. A neurotic person, however, is willing to consider one or two of these questions, but has broken down in face of some new and overwhelming reverse.

The cases I have been describing exhibit such incomplete stoppage. In the one immediately under consideration, the girl appeared to be quite healthy until she suffered the setback in her occupation. Then, more deeply intimidated by the difficulty of life, she began to shelve its problems more and more, and strove for a new kind of superiority in the form of compulsion-ideas.

One day she had a fear that her handbag had come open and that some coins, covered with verdigris, had dropped into the basket of vegetables which she had been carrying for another woman. She feared she had poisoned this woman's entire family ! Another compulsion-idea that she had, was that the dust of the street was on her hands and would soil her mother's Bible if she touched it, which of course she could not avoid doing from time to time. So after each imaginary soiling of the Bible she surreptitiously bought another and replaced it, till she had bought a dozen of them. She attributed this exaggerated holiness to the books in order that she might profane them ; and wasted her money on them so that she could be held irresponsible. Thus also, she became a martyr, misunderstood, and a soul degraded by the fouling of sacred things.

If the girl's sole ambition in life had been to become more conspicuous than her sister, she was well on the way to realise it. But this neurotic aim was involving her in such practical defeats that it was clearly advisable for her to renounce it for another. The goal of her striving was to escape the dreaded decision—" My sister is superior to me."

Closely examined, this escape from a decision also reveals

itself as a goal of superiority. As she will not mix with people she cannot be defeated socially. As long as she avoids love and marriage she is not measured with her sister's happy marriage. Whatever happens, she can say— " But then I am fully occupied with my compulsion-ideas." She must be occupied with something. Time, the circumstances, and whatever logic her neurosis has not destroyed, demand some occupation, so she busies herself on the useless side with this compulsion-neurosis. Her activity is actually free from competition, and fictitiously superior. This illusion of superiority is shown by her striving, in compulsion-ideas, to make herself feel responsible for the lives of others, or for their purity. This effort to show a superior conscientiousness is her occupation, for she has not stopped. If she had, she would be in a state of stupor, as in catatonia.

Before referring to this patient's dreams a few general remarks are advisable. A psychology which could not understand and interpret dreams would exclude a great part of the mental life, and would therefore be a most imperfect psychology. Thus the Freudian conception of dreams is an important contribution. Unfortunately its author overlooked the most vital principles of dream-formation owing to his mistaken assumption of the dominance of the sexual factor. This prevented him from seeing that the sexual attitude in life is determined by the goal of totality or superiority. We must always interpret abnormal sexual tendencies as expressions of the entire style of life, looking for the deeper movements which underlie them.

The understanding of dreams owes its furthest practical

progress to a contribution of Individual Psychology—the recognition, namely, that every dream creates its *mood*. To cope with a specific situation, in accordance with the goal of superiority, the dream insinuates a mood. This alone explains the mysterious fact that people do not understand their own dreams. Dreaming is a process of turning away, in sleep, from reality and common sense towards the individual's goal of superiority. To relate our present problems to this goal by logical planning and thinking is very difficult ; but by the feelings it is easy, and their " short cut " is the dream.

As I have shown elsewhere, the dream is a dress rehearsal, a trial performance of a step towards the fictive goal. It produces, in an automatic way, an illusory picture of how to succeed in disregard of the logic of the situation.

This patient dreamt that she fell down. No one can deny that such a dream connotes unpleasant feelings as of defeat, and we could not but assume that she was diminishing her impulse to proceed. Presumably there was a present question which she wanted to answer in a discouraged manner. That present question proved to be an invitation by the married man in the case, to a *rendezvous*. She responded by giving herself, through the dream, the hopeless mood she wanted—the impulse to denial and escape.

In case the critical reader is unconvinced, I will cite another dream of the patient's upon the same night. She was terrified by noticing some blue and red spots on her skin. Was this a good preparation for a meeting with a lover ? That the spots signified the result of a luetic infection was not only obvious to me but was suggested quite independently by the patient herself. In discussing this matter she expressed the opinion that all men were untrue and polygamous. " I am sure," she exclaimed—and this I have already quoted—" that my husband would leave me a fort-night after the wedding. What is the good of marriage, if I constantly expect to be deceived and also infected by my husband ? " This clinches the proof of her motive to escape. She added, " I should become less than my sister, whose husband is faithful." Thus her goal has changed. She no longer wishes directly to surpass her sister, but barricades that way, and looks for another superiority—on the useless side. She was going to avoid all defeat, and to be nobler than anyone else.

———————

Everyone's goal is one of superiority, but in the case of those who lose their courage and self-confidence, it is diverted from the useful to the useless side of life. This escape into a life of unrealities takes place in an automatic way : the fear of defeat itself arranges the emotions, and through them the actions, until a situation is reached which allays it. This escape is always felt as a relief, but is not understood as such. If it were, the patient would enjoy it, which would spoil the whole arrangement by removing the justification for his hesitation and escape. He must pay the costs with suffering in order to be excusable. And the neurotic symptoms, being built upon the pattern of an illness, really resemble illness, and efficiently safeguard the patient's sense of superiority by enabling him to think, " I could be the first if my suffering did not postpone it." From such a style of life happiness is excluded *a priori* and quite independently of any adjustment to circumstances.

II

Inability to Meet the Problems of Life

A SCHIZOPHRENIC BOY

EVERY development in an individual's life is conditioned by his life-aim, by which the successive phases of his life are organically connected. When a mother, whose son has suddenly become schizophrenic at the age of eighteen, says that he was perfectly normal until that age, we cannot agree with her. And we find, upon enquiry into the boy's past life, that he was of a domineering disposition and did not play with his schoolmates. Such a childhood is a bad preparation for facing the real problems of life. In this case it was a preparation for schizophrenia, which was not a sudden development but the result of a life-attitude, and only showed itself when he had to face a really difficult situation. At the age of eighteen he was faced with the three questions of society, occupation, and love, and felt unable to answer them. A patient's unpreparedness for life does not always show itself in favourable circumstances, nor when he is shielded from the real demands of life, which are always of a social nature and demand social feeling. Childhood is normally a sheltered period of life, but it may be passed in such a way that the social feeling is undeveloped, as it was in the case under consideration and also in the case previously described where a girl was in competition with an elder sister, felt her prestige endangered all the time and was therefore preoccupied with herself. Such a conception of its situation hinders a child's development of social feeling.

The circumstances of early life, such as those of the nursery, kindergarten, school, and companionship, are the first training and test in social behaviour.   When a neurosis is developed we always find that the individual's difficulties were foreshadowed in these relations of childhood.   He did not care to do things with others, or he did so with some queer or noticeable difference from others.   And a neurotic generally remembers his peculiarities and difficulties of adaptation in early life as a justification for keeping his distance from the present social environment.   When he is driven by necessity or by his own demands, to approach more nearly to an accepted standard of behaviour, the neurotic may apparently try to adapt himself, but in reality he does nothing of the kind : he answers the new demands with automatic responses and trained attitudes of long standing under cover of which he escapes from any real contact.   He may mix with others superficially, in conversation and customary kinds of co-operation, but he does so according to his own established mechanisms, and behind this screen his psyche slips back into its own secret stronghold.   In this behaviour of neurotics, psychotics, and problem-children we must recognise a certain inevitability, a necessary result of their past.   The artificial attitudes which they have elaborated are the logical consequence of faulty training, and we can do very little good by trying to correct these consequences.   We must make a change in the deeper motive, in the underlying style of life, and then the patient will see all his life-tasks in a new perspective.

The three problems of life which I have already described must be solved somehow or other by every human being, for the individual's relation with the world is a three-fold relation. No one can escape a definite answer to the question of society, or of occupation, or of sex. And whoever can make friends with society, can pursue a useful occupation with faith and courage, and can adjust his sexual life in accordance with good social feeling, is immune from neurotic infection. But when an individual fails to square himself with one or more of these three inexorable demands of life, beware of feelings of abasement, beware of the consequent neurosis. Schizophrenia is the result of a failure in all three directions at once.

The boy whose case we are considering was unprepared to grapple with these inevitable problems. From our point of view, it is evident that he needed re-education at this late stage of his development, a process which demands a special method. It is well for the practitioner to realise at the outset that nothing can be done by force. The patient must be appealed to in a friendly way, coaxed into a receptive frame of mind. Indeed, the task of the physician or psychologist is to give the patient the experience of contact with a fellow-man, and then to enable him to transfer this awakened social feeling to others.

— — — — — —

This method, of winning the patient's good will, and then transferring it to his environment, is strictly analogous to the maternal function. The social duty of motherhood is to interpret society to the individual, and if the mother fails in this the duty is likely to devolve much later upon the physician who is heavily handicapped for the task. The mother has the enormous advantage of the physical and psychic relation ; she is the greatest experience of love and fellowship that the child will ever have. Her duty is mentally to relate the growing child to herself, as it was formerly related to her physically, nourishing the child's growing consciousness with true and normal conceptions of society, of work, and of love. In this way she gradually transforms the child's love for her and dependence upon her into a benevolent, confident, and responsible attitude towards society and the whole environment. This is the two-fold function of motherhood, to give the child the completest possible experience of human fellowship, and then to widen it into a life-attitude towards others.

AN ELDERLY WOMAN'S EXCESSIVE GLOOM

It is always after a prolonged struggle to hold one's ground that what we call psychosis is liable to supervene. The individual then breaks down before all the three questions of life, and every step he takes is made in defiance of logic.

In this connection, what we mean by logical is that which is intelligible as an attempt to *solve* a real problem of life. An example of psychotic development may be given in the life of an elderly woman, excluded from occupation and from love. She is offended because society, her children and sons-in-law do not take enough interest in her. If she has not developed sufficient social feeling to take a keen interest in the lives of others, her case is indeed a difficult one ; for the goal of superiority still attracts her as much as anyone, and keeps her striving without any definite object- ive. But she finds it possible to impress others by exploit- ing her weakness. She can become a focus of attention again, and once more an actress on the stage of life, by taking up the rôle of an entirely hopeless person. She will forestall the destruction of her personality by identifying herself with a lost person, and, rather than allow that others should make her miserable by neglect she will plunge herself into excessive gloom, a procedure which also gives her a little dismal power over other people's feelings. We find that the pride and ambition of neurotic persons prohibits their confessing that they feel neglected, so that they are unable directly to accuse others. The anger and rage which we should expect to find in this phase of life is, therefore, generally suppressed and hidden, though it may break out occasionally, and they rationalise their hopeless attitude by turning all their accusation against themselves. In cases of melancholia many persons actually kill themselves, in an excess of self-condemnation, while sometimes ostentatiously exonerating others.

THE DOMINATING WIFE WITH MELANCHOLIA

A very intelligent woman, forty-six years of age, had suffered from melancholia for three years, eight years before she came to me. She had been married at the age of sixteen, and having no children for the first ten years of her married life, she adopted a child, but did not tell the child that she was not its real mother. This situation is one which usually leads to unhappiness for the child later on. Afterwards the woman had two daughters of her own. She worked in her husband's office after marriage, so that she knew all about his affairs, and when, after some years, he took a partner into his business, she did not care to be in the office because of her diminished importance. She quarrelled continually with the partner until her father fell ill, when she withdrew from the business to nurse him, and as soon as the father's health was restored she developed melancholia. She suspected her husband of concealing his business affairs from her, and cried if he did not immediately tell her everything she wanted to know. She wanted to dominate her husband, and crying was a means by which she sought to subdue him. Crying is usually an accusation against another person. Her husband's business was financially satisfactory, and it was not necessary for her to know all the details of its working, but she felt herself excluded and inferior if she did not know all about it.

This was a strong woman who had married a weak man in order to rule him, and, of course, the choice of an equal mate generally indicates a higher degree of courage. Marriage is a constructive task for two persons who are determined to live together in order to relieve and to enrich each other's lives ; and when anyone chooses a weaker partner—lower in the social scale, or with vices such as alcoholism, morphinism, or laziness—in the hope of " saving " him, he betrays the hidden desire for superiority.

This woman showed the principal signs of a true melancholia. She decreased steadily in weight, was unable to sleep, and was always more depressed in the morning than in the evening. She feared that the whole family would come to poverty and starvation. In treating the case my first objective was to reconcile her with her husband. I tried to show her that her husband was getting older, that she should not be angry with him, but handle him more diplomatically   I explained that there were better methods of making him subservient than crying ; that the weaker always puts up some kind of resistance, as no one can endure constant domination, and that people must treat each other as equals if they are to live harmoniously together.

I always use the simplest and most direct method possible in the treatment of neurotics, but it would be of no use to tell the patient in this case, " You are a domineering woman, and you are now trying to rule by means of illness," for she would be offended. I must win her first, and take her part as far as possible. Every neurotic is partly in the right. If this woman did not feel deprived of value by her advancing age—a real privation of women in our present culture—she would not cling to her prestige in such unseemly ways. But it is only very gradually that I can bring her to face the truth about what she is doing.

At the same time this patient developed a guilt complex— which often happens in such a situation. She remembered that she had deceived her husband with another man some twenty-five years before, during all which time this event had played no further part in her life, but all at once she told her husband and accused herself. This so-called guilt-complex, which we should wholly misunderstand by the Freudian interpretation, was quite clearly an attack upon the husband who was no longer obedient. She could hurt him by confession and self-accusation. Who is so simple as to think that it is a case of the majesty of the truth vindicating itself after a quarter of a century ? The truth is often a terrible weapon of aggression. It is possible to lie, and even to murder, with the truth.

Nietzsche, with a most penetrating vision and from the same standpoint as we take for Individual Psychology, described the feeling of guilt as mere wickedness. And in the majority of neurotic cases the fact is that a guilt complex is used as a means to fix its maker on the useless side of life.

This is often seen in the case of a child, who tells a lie and gets a complex about it, by which arrangement he can play a rôle of distinguished uselessness. Everyone will be struck by his honesty if he worries so much about having told a fib.

—————

To return to the indirect method of treatment : I recommend it especially in melancholia. After establishing a sympathetic relation I give suggestions for a change of conduct in two stages. In the first stage my suggestion is " Only do what is agreeable to you." The patient usually answers, " Nothing is agreeable." " Then at least," I respond, " do not exert yourself to do what is disagreeable." The patient, who has usually been exhorted to do various uncongenial things to remedy his condition, finds a rather flattering novelty in my advice, and may improve in behaviour. Later I insinuate the second rule of conduct, saying that " it is much more difficult and I do not know if you can follow it." After saying this I am silent, and look doubtfully at the patient. In this way I excite his curiosity and ensure his attention, and then proceed, " If you could follow this second rule you would be cured in fourteen days. It is—to consider from time to time how you can give another person pleasure. It would very soon enable you to sleep and would chase away all your sad thoughts. You would feel yourself to be useful and worth while."

I receive various replies to my suggestion, but every patient thinks it is too difficult to act upon. If the answer is, " How can I give pleasure to others when I have none myself ? " I relieve the prospect by saying, " Then you will need four weeks." The more transparent response, " Who gives *me* pleasure ? " I encounter with what is probably the strongest move in the game, by saying, " Perhaps you had better train yourself a little thus : do not actually *do* anything to please anyone else, but just think out how you *could* do it."

Melancholy subjects who reply, " Oh, that is quite easy ; it is what I have always done," are to be suspected of dispensing favours in order to get the upper hand of others. To them I say, " Do you think the people you favoured were really pleased by it ? "   I sometimes give in, admitting that it is too difficult at present because the patient needs practice and training, by which compromise I carry a milder measure in these terms :—" Remember all the ideas you have in the night, and give *me* pleasure by telling them to me the next day."

The next day such a patient quite probably replies, " I slept all night," when asked for his midnight reflections, even though he had not previously slept for many days ! But let the physician beware lest he triumph too soon.   He should continue industriously to collect all the useful facts and reconstruct the patient's style of life.

In treating these cases I have never had a suicide, the disaster which so commonly occurs, and I believe this is due to the fact that this indirect treatment reduces the acute tension.   But all those who are in the patient's environment must be made to understand that they cannot scold, force, or criticise, but must assist the patient into a more favourable situation.   Melancholia is an illness in which the people in the environment suffer more than the patient, and there are moments when the relatives can no longer endure the strain.   My advice is, " Five minutes before you feel you can no longer control the patient, put him in charge of one or two attendants."   This is the phase in which suicide is threatening.

Mania, in common with melancholia and the severer neuroses, is a barricade erected by the patient to block his own approach to the real business of life, and it is sometimes preliminary to the establishment of psychosis in the form of manic-depressive insanity. The first formidable phase of mental disorder, as we have seen, is invariably when some urgent problem presses for solution and the patient has lost courage. In mania there is an effort to overcome this cowardice of the soul, and the patient pushes himself forward, exaggerates his actions, and talks and laughs with needless excitement. He is high-spirited and irritable, has great projects, is very superior and boastful of his power, and displays strong sexual inclinations. These patients need watching or they may do damage, but this phase of their illness is a sudden blaze which soon consumes its fuel. The natural and usual sequel is a phase of melancholia in which the patient must on no account be restrained as he barricades himself from expression all too surely. Such alternations in manic-depressive insanity are shown by individuals who showed slight phases of conduct of the same pattern in their earlier life. They begin with an excitement which rapidly wanes into a depression. This tendency is shown even in their handwriting, in which the first letter of a word is written very large, while the others decrease in size and droop below the line. Brilliant beginnings and sudden anti-climaxes are repeated at intervals throughout their life-histories.

Manic-depressive insanity, like a cyclothymia beginning late in life, may yield an appearance so similar to general paralysis as to cause confusion in diagnosis. In such a case the clinical symptoms must be supplemented by an examination of the spinal fluid. This is important, as there are many cases of only a single attack of paralysis, whereas cyclothymea is, of course, recurrent. I once had a patient of this kind whose mania stopped very quickly. I was visiting him at the asylum when he begged me to take him home, as the attendants had treated him roughly a few days before. He had begun to recover and his condition was improving every hour, so I took him home. As we sat down at table he remarked with satisfaction, " You see, it has always been like this in my life. I have always got whatever I wanted." While I was thinking only of the hard knocks he had suffered, he was thinking of nothing but having got out of the asylum. That is the difference between the objectivity of common sense and the sort of " private intelligence " which is the basis of mania.

III

Lack of Social Feeling, and Masculine Protest

INDIVIDUAL Psychology distinguishes in the conscious and the unconscious, not separate and conflicting entities, but complementary and co-operating parts of one and the same reality. That reality is not of a physiological or biological nature, and it eludes any chemical or technical tests. The fact that anxiety, for instance, affects the sympathetic and para-sympathetic nerves does not reveal the cause of an anxiety. The origin of anxiety is in the psychic and not in the somatic realm : we attribute it neither to the suppression of sexuality nor to the conditions of childhood, although we have given all due importance to these factors. What appears to us most important is such a fact as this, for instance ; that a child will make use of anxiety in order to arrive at its goal of superiority— of *control* over the mother. The most exact physiological and neurological description of anger appears to us to be of almost negligible practical value compared with our actual experience of how anger is used to dominate a person or a situation. In this respect we claim to have taken up the only standpoint which is correctly and purely a psychological one ; 'and we believe that the ascription of feelings, emotions and thoughts to bodily conditions and inherited instincts—which is the basis of almost all other psychologies—always leads to exaggerations and mistakes. We are far from disputing that every mental and bodily function is necessarily conditioned by inherited material, but what we see in all psychic activity is the *use which is made* of this material to attain a certain goal. In all the cases I have hitherto described, the feelings and emotions were developed in the direction and to the degree required for the attainment of a particular goal, which in these instances was of neurotic character. Anxiety, sadness, and every other manifestation took the line we could have predicted from the style of life ; and we have seen how dreams also played their part in arranging the feelings into conformity with the general striving, their action giving us a remarkable insight into the workshop of the soul.

If sadness is necessary to the attainment of his goal, an individual is naturally incapable of happiness, for he can only be happy when miserable. But we notice that feelings appear and disappear as required. A person suffering from agoraphobia loses the feeling of anxiety when at home, or when he successfully subdues another person to himself. The tendency of the neurotic is to exclude from his experience the whole sphere of life *except* those parts of it in which he has the sense of being a conqueror. By manufacturing certain moods or emotions in himself he finds he can repel and shut out the undesirable, unconquerable remainder of his world. He even comes vainly to hide his head in the moods themselves, like an ostrich.

Beneath all fluctuations of mood, however, and ruling them, lies the real character, which is relatively unchangeable. A coward, for example, even though he shows arrogance against a weaker person or courage in a shielded position, still remains a coward ; and his freedom from

anxiety, when surrounded by watchdogs, guns and policemen, does not deceive us. His character is indicated by
the excessive protection he demands. The proud man may
even be very gracious and yielding, but we note that he
surrounds himself by inferiors. To estimate the true
character of an individual we must always give full significance to the environment he has chosen or permitted for
himself.

That which we call social feeling in Individual Psychology
is the true and inevitable compensation for all the natural
weaknesses of individual human beings. The human being,
even biologically considered, is clearly a social being,
needing a much longer period of dependence upon others
before its maturity than any animal : and the human
mother also is more dependent before, during, and after
giving birth. The high degree of co-operation and social
culture which man needs for his very existence demands
spontaneous social effort, and the dominant purpose of
education is to evoke it. Social feeling is not inborn ; but
it is an innate potentiality which has to be consciously
developed. We are unable to trust any so-called social
" instinct," for its expression depends upon the child's
conception or vision of the environment. In the growth of
this vision of society the most vital factor is the mother,
as we have seen, for it is *in its mother that every child makes
its first contact with a trustworthy fellow-man*. In the four or
five earliest years of life the child builds up its own prototype, by adjusting its inherited abilities to its earliest
impressions, and lays the irrevocable foundation of its style
of life. It is this which develops later into the more formu-

lated life-style, and conditions the answers to the three questions of life. In the former, or earliest period, the psychic soundness of the mother is what is essential; in the second period, her mentality and breadth of outlook are very important.

The mother brings about the first important and specifically human change in the child's behaviour. Under her influence the child first inhibits its desires and organic impulses, and introduces delays and circuitous methods into its striving for what it wants. The goal of all striving, which is to overcome the difficulties of life and to gain superiority, is also the stimulus of childhood, which begins with a sense of almost total practical impotence. It is the attentive, benevolent mother who is, to the child, the guardian of its goal—even largely the goal itself in concrete form. But such a goal is not permanently possible : and the art of motherhood is to give the child freedom and opportunity for success by its own efforts, so that it can establish its style of life and seek for its superiority in increasingly useful ways. Then gradually she must interest the child in other persons and in the wider environment of life. So far as she can discharge these two functions—of bestowing independence and of imparting a true initial understanding of the surrounding situation in the home and in the world— she will see the child develop social feeling, independence, and courage. And so far also will the child find its own goal in being a fellow-man and friend, a good worker and a true partner in love. With such an initiation into life, the ineradicable will to superiority is united with social feeling, and issues in courageous and optimistic activity upon the useful side of life. All the feelings of an individual, throughout his life, are modified by the amount of communal feeling that is involved in his individual striving for prestige.

Every kind of action upon the useless side of life, such as the behaviour of problem-children, neurotics, criminals, sexual perverts, prostitutes, and suicides, can be more or less precisely traced to lack of social feeling, with the consequent loss of confidence. For we must realise that every adaptation we have to make in life, from kindergarten to business management, from school chums to marriage is, directly or indirectly, a social action. From the earliest times, we face new thoughts and events in a manner which is dominantly social or antisocial, it cannot be neutral. Suppose, for instance, that a boy is terrified by illness and death in his environment. He may allay his fears by the determination to be a doctor, and to fight against death. This is obviously a more social idea than that of being a grave-digger, the one who buries the *others*—a reaction which I have also found in a boy in that situation. When social feeling has been from the first instilled into the upward strivings of the psyche it acts with automatic certainty, colouring every thought and action, and where this automatised social feeling is deficient, the individual's interest is too self-centred, and he feels that he is impotent or a nobody. With this feeling all his other feelings are more or less directly connected : they do not exist *sui generis*, nor do they control action, although they are often used to do so—and, of course, they influence our secondary decisions from time to time.

The sense of impotence, or the " feeling of inferiority," is the root-conception of Individual Psychology. Whatever form it may take, it can only be correctly estimated from an adequate study of the individual's *actions*. Its accurate diagnosis is perhaps more difficult in early life, where we see many efforts to circumvent the instincts and to conceal the feeling itself from its possessor, but most of these early expressions are connected with the strength or weakness of the organs and the friendliness or hostility of the environment. Yet neither the inherited organism nor the environment is wholly responsible for the sense of impotence, nor is it caused by both together. The degree to which it is felt is due to both these factors *plus* the reaction of the child. As a conscious relation between its organism and environment, the child's psyche seems to have an indefinite *causal* power : so that, normal or abnormal, it never reacts with anything like mathematical exactitude. Life, as opposed to dead material, always reacts thus, in a more or less inaccurate—and spontaneous—manner.

For convenience, however, we may classify certain typical variations of the sense of impotence, according to typical causes. Thus there are three types of neurotic children—those with defective organs, those who are spoiled and those who are hated. Physical defects, whether congenital or acquired, invariably cause feelings of inferiority, and we can generally trace a special effort to compensate for the specific defect. For example, many who are naturally left-handed and who have been trained to use the right hand only, conceal their sense of manual inadequacy by taking to the arts. Extreme dexterity and finesse of handling such as that of an instrumentalist or a painter, becomes an integral factor in their life-goal. There are also many painters and poets whose choice of their vocation was influenced by bad eyesight. Milton and Homer are conspicuous examples of this latter compensation. In the deafness of Beethoven and in the stuttering of Demosthenes also, we see the points upon which their strivings were concentrated.

Many persons have resented the attention that I and my colleagues have drawn to this compensatory factor in the work of artists of genius or of high talent, and they attempt to deny what our experience is constantly confirming. But their objection is due to a misunderstanding of the findings of Individual Psychology. We are not so foolish as to suppose that organic imperfection is the efficient cause of genius. Many of the Freudians have indeed supposed that the sublimest works of human genius were directly caused by sexual repressions, but we make no such eccentric generalisation. In our view, a man of genius is primarily a man of supreme usefulness. If he is an artist he is useful to culture, giving distinction and value by his work to the recreative life of many thousands. And this value, where it is genuine, and not merely empty brilliance, depends upon a high degree of courage and communal intuition. The *origin* of genius lies neither in the inherited organism nor in the environmental influences, but in that third sphere of individual reaction to which I have already referred, which includes the possibility of socially affirmative action. In the choice of its specialised *expression*, however, the highest talent is conditioned by the organism with which it is endowed, from the greatest *defect* of which it gains its particular mode of concentration.

A knowledge of this principle, which can only be rightly gained by much observation, is of the greatest service in the treatment of organically defective children, as it enables us to protect them from many dangers of over-compensation.

The spoiled child, being in a position where it receives too much from others, never proves its own powers to itself. Its goal, formed in accordance with its experience, is to be the centre of the family, the focus of attention and care. The usual symptoms are : anger, discontent, disorderliness, anxiety, enuresis, a struggle to avoid isolation, and unwillingness to go to school. Treatment readily suggests itself ; but we have often to take into account a quite unusually intense feeling of insecurity.

The hated child is in the worse position of never having been spoiled by anyone. Its goal is to escape and to get at a safe distance from others. Cruelty, slyness, and cowardliness are some of the symptoms. Such a child is often unable to look one straight in the eyes, cannot speak, and hides its feelings in fear of abasement. Its constant tendency to find fault may in some instances be developed in the direction of useful criticism.

No soul develops in freedom. Each one is in mental, emotional and nutritive dependence upon his immediate environment on the earth and in the cosmos, yet so far independent that he must take up these relations consciously : he must answer them as the questions of life. Everything he does is an answer—no doubt it is the best he can give. We are not blest with omniscience, and our greatest reasonable hope is not to answer with a great mistake, so that we had better test all views, including that of Individual Psychology, and prove them carefully. Our best science must be applied with common sense.

Hated children also take life as they find it, respond to it with the best reactions they can devise, and gradually *fix* these reactions into a mechanical pattern of life. The three life-problems, in whatever successive forms they present themselves, will thenceforward be encountered by that fixed *pattern* of behaviour, however it may be elaborated by experience. The unusual tension of their life makes these children postulate a higher goal of security and superiority than that of the average child. All their impressions, perceptions and attitudes are conditioned by the perspective of their prejudiced situation : so that what they learn from life is seldom any new aspect but only how to fill in the old one with more detail.

In these three types of children we encounter the three typical accentuations of the feeling of inferiority. They all weaken the social contact, and tend to isolate the individual in an ever-narrowing sphere of interest. Unsocial types take on very deceptive appearances at times. I once called to see an old lady I knew, who was well known for benevolent actions, and found her crying while an old man, also in tears, stood before her. " What is the matter ? " I asked. " Look at this poor old man," she sobbed. " He has five starving children, and is to be turned out of his house if he doesn't pay the ten shillings he owes—and I have only five to give him ! " " Don't cry," I replied " Let me add to your generous gift a little gift of five shillings." She thanked me effusively, saying she had always known me to be a good man. Now I knew that this old lady was not only very rich but she had no real social interest, she consorted only with her own relatives, and even with them in a very dominating spirit. Her charitable action was no contradiction to her character : her pity and sadness over this poor man gave her the kind of feeling of superiority she lived for. It is of no use to judge an isolated demonstration of feeling, apart from the whole style of life.

For a psychological understanding we must perceive the goal towards which all the feelings tend.

A BOY WITH OBSESSIVE GUILT FEELINGS

I have already called attention to the use of guilt feelings in building up a neurotic and imaginary superiority. One of the clearest examples in my experience was the case of a boy, the second child in the family, whose father and elder brother were both notable for honesty of character. As is usual with second children, this boy's striving was largely concentrated upon the effort to surpass the elder brother. At the age of seven he lied to his teacher, pretending that a piece of work in which his brother had helped him, was all his own. This gave him a feeling of guilt which he concealed for three years, after which he went to the teacher and confessed that he had lied. The teacher refused to take the matter seriously, but only laughed, so the boy went and unburdened himself to his father, with great emotion and sadness. The father was gratified by what he took to be a profound love of truth, and consoled and praised his son. But the boy's depression did not vanish with this paternal absolution. He continued to think, with a neurotic compulsion, that he was a liar. The high moral atmosphere of the home, and the feeling that he was worse than his brother, both in school work and in popularity, had combined to set him striving for excellence in the supreme family virtue. He was secretly dedicated to proving even by the life-long expiation of a trifling transgression, that his integrity was greater than any one's.

The boy's neurosis developed. He acquired other self-reproaches, for not being entirely honest in work and, as is usual, for masturbation. These always became most acute just before an examination. By amassing difficulties in this way he felt excused for not surpassing his brother. He planned a course of technical training after leaving the university, but by that time his compulsion neurosis had increased so much that most of his time was employed in prayer to God to forgive him, which, of course, put work out of the question. He was admitted to an asylum, where they supposed him incurable, but his condition improved and he left the asylum, asking, however, to be re-admitted if he should have a relapse. At this point he changed his occupation and began to study the history of art. Before sitting for an examination in this subject, however, he put it beyond the bounds of possibility by a piece of extraordinary behaviour. He went to church on a special day of festival, when the building was crowded, and prostrated himself publicly, crying out that he was the greatest of sinners.

In this striking achievement of a central position in a large public assembly, we can detect an ambition of the same pattern as he had in childhood. To be the greatest penitent among all the worshippers in a church is the same kind of distinction as to have the softest conscience for a lie in a family of supreme honesty. It is to be better than the best. He made another exhibition of himself when he returned to the asylum, by coming to lunch one day entirely naked. He was a well-built man and quite equal to the rest of his family in bodily appearance.

This patient's escape from work and examinations was due to fear that he would not shine in these normal situations. The guilty feeling, specially intensified when required, must be regarded as an intentional exclusion of activities in which he had no confidence of success. There was also a tendency to score a cheap success of notoriety which is not at all out of keeping with his general aim, and it was this which prompted him to appear naked at the meal, and to other eccentricities of behaviour.

——————

The task of the physician is to enable such a patient to realise what he is doing, and to transfer his egocentric interest to social life and useful activity. This is an art, in which the Individual Psychologist must train himself by practice and collaboration, for science and the knowledge of principles alone will never enable him to win the complete confidence which is required. In the case I have just described, for example, I had to recognise correctly, in the first quarter of an hour of the patient's visit, the kind of superiority for which this style of life was designed. If I had failed to do so I should certainly have provoked prompt resistance. Step by step I had to induce his correct statement of his difficulties in childhood, to make him reveal, with less and less reluctance, his deep feelings of worthlessness compared with his brother. Then it was easier for him to admit to himself how he impressed his father with his honesty and how he had manœuvred himself into limelight positions.

The method of Individual Psychology, because it requires the admission and correction of mistakes still dear to the patient, involves the utmost art and craft of the practitioner. We are far from denying that other schools of psychiatry have their successes in dealing with neuroses, but in our experience they do so less by their methods than when they happen to give the patient a good human relation with the physician, or above all, to give him encouragement. It is a fact that a quack or an osteopath sometimes improves a person's attitude to life to a considerable extent ; so also may a St. Anne de Beaupré, a Christian Scientist, or a Coué, or a visit to Lourdes. But we remain convinced that the cure of all mental disorder lies in the simpler, if more laborious process of making the patient understand his own mistakes.

As we have already seen, the style of life of most of our patients can be traced to three typical positions of inferiority in childhood. There are certain mistakes of adaptation which prevent the establishment of a normal style of life, and which are evident even before the child faces its first social problems beyond the home. One of these mistakes of childhood is a refusal to accept the sexual rôle, in which case a boy grows up like a girl—or *vice versa.*

Such errors are very common, and indeed nearly everyone shows some slight tendencies towards them. Perhaps every man has something in either body or behaviour which we feel to be feminine, and women often have very masculine traits of a physical character without always showing a corresponding masculinity of mind. More often, however, the wrong sexuality is in the mind and not in the body.

The sex glands, it is true, have an extensive influence on the body. But they have a very limited power to determine the individual's conception of superiority. It is this individual goal of supremacy which is chiefly responsible for a person's confusion about his true sexual function. When we are dealing with the mental symptoms of inverted sexuality we must remember this and not blame too much upon the glands. It is probably equally true that the mental striving affects the glands themselves in the long run. We must see first of all how the patient relates his ideas of sexuality to his goal.

A YOUNG WOMAN WHO ALWAYS WANTED TO BE A BOY

The goal of superiority is always more or less identified with the masculine rôle owing to the privileges, both real and imaginary, with which our present civilisation has invested the male. A girl's feeling of inferiority may be markedly increased when she realises that she is a female, and a boy's also when he doubts his maleness. Both compensate by an exaggeration of what they imagine to be masculine behaviour. This form of compensation, which may have the most varied and intricate consequences according to circumstances, is what I have called the *masculine protest*. Its chief symptom both in mind and in outward conduct is a needlessly domineering attitude towards the opposite sex It is always noticeably connected with a very ambitious style of life, with a goal of super-man or of a very much pampered woman. The behaviour is over-strained, a fact which may be veiled in favourable situations but is revealed clearly in times of defeat. The masculine protest is indicated to a certain degree in some of the cases I have quoted, but I will give a more typical instance.

A neurotic woman, twenty-six years old, who came to consult me, had lost her mother at six, after which she lived with an indulgent father until she was thirteen. Her earliest memory was : " I hated to play with dolls." This was a sign of her unwillingness to develop in a normal manner : she preferred to play with toy railway-trains. She always wanted to be wild in conduct, and only played with boys, like a typical hoyden. If she did play with girls, she pulled their hair and annoyed them in other ways. To my question, " What do you think about men and women ? " she replied, " Women are always intriguing ; men are straightforward." This is a still more definite sign of a will towards masculine development.

In parenthesis, I may say that I should never forbid a girl to play with trains, to climb trees, or to play any boys' games, but I am fully convinced that much trouble would be saved in the later life of children if they were brought up from the first in knowledge and preparation for their right sexual rôle. This is impossible, of course, if the atmosphere is charged with suggestions of feminine disability and of masculine privilege, as so often is the case.

All those who disesteem women as a sex incur certain punishment, because they develop an attitude which is in contradiction to truth and reality.

I asked my patient to tell me about her feelings towards men and women. She said that when she was thirteen she laughed when she heard that persons fell in love. She knew nothing of love until her twentieth year. This, together with the fact that she was a keen athlete, confirmed the ostrich-like flight from her sexual rôle : she wanted to laugh love out of the question and to deny her feminity by excelling in athletics. I expected to find difficulty in menstruation, which is often experienced by girls who have a grudge against their feminine nature, giving them great pain and tendencies to anger, but this was not the case with her. At the age of thirteen, when her indulgent father married again, one would have expected her to show signs of anger, but she did not. She scorned to do anything so womanly, but said she was glad her father was married so that she could be free. However, trouble with her father began from that time, and she fought in the home, saying that she wanted to be free to leave home and to become a social worker. She wanted to conquer her father by financial independence. Her desire to be a social worker was coloured by the thought of ruling over children

We are familiar, of course, with the desire that patients so often express, not to take any money from their families. When a patient tells me he does not intend to take any more money from his family I often say : " Better take it. It will be cheaper for them in the end."

This patient had many men friends, but was never in love. It is usual for boys and girls to fall in love about twelve or thirteen, and not uncommon when they are five or six. An individual who reaches the age of twenty-three without any such experience is not prepared for it. Love is a necessary life-task for which an early preparation is needed, and training for love is an integral part of one's education for life. Both normal love and all its perversions such as homosexuality are a matter of training and education.

At the age of twenty-three this girl had a feeling which she thought was love ; she liked a man better than she had ever liked anyone before, and the affair led to intercourse. This free sex-relation was a part of her striving for independence, expressing her opposition to her father, and her determination to be manlike. The man's feelings changed, and he disappeared for a time. Unable to bear this defeat the girl tried to follow him, with the result one might expect in our civilisation, where men are taught to think it *infra dig.* to be wooed, and are afraid of having it too easily. The man cooled off more and more, and she saw him at last with another girl, for which she reproached him, and in quarrel with her the man told her she was a common girl. After this he disappeared entirely and married the other one.

For some time after this my patient only kept up her

sporting and athletic relations with men, and was frightened if they made any other advances : she ran away when a man friend wanted to kiss her. Later on she became the mistress of a second man, but she was unhappy, fought with him constantly, and would not consent to marry him. The man took a voyage to Africa, thinking it would be better to absent himself for a while, but her unhappiness continued, and was now fraught with memories of her first lover. In her continual quarrels we see her excuse for not marrying, as also in her return to the image of the married and therefore unattainable lover. A typical symptom was that sex relations did not satisfy her. She had not been prepared for marriage.

To this girl the thought of being a woman was identified with defeat. Thus, if she behaved like a girl and considered the prospect of marriage, she could not endure it ; it was easier to go on playing at being a boy by keeping up her athletic pursuits. On the other hand she felt that marriage was a natural and logical social demand. In this conflicting situation she was further discouraged by two great defeats : firstly, by her father, when he ceased to spoil her and married again, and secondly, by the desertion of her first lover. To safeguard herself against another defeat she put love and marriage at the greatest possible distance, and to justify her halt before this problem and to ensure it, she persuaded herself that it was impossible for a girl to keep a man's love. The fundamental difficulty in this case, as in many others, was the idea that the feminine function is of definitely second-rate importance, and therefore not really worth while. This is one of the chief causes of unhappiness in love and marriage, and it is the illusion which is the basis of the masculine protest.

IV

Problems of Love and Marriage

At the end of all my lectures I have to reply to questions about love and marriage, and my questioners often appear to have been misled by some psychological reading into believing that the sexual impulse is the central motive to which every other activity is related. I have never seen the reason for placing this unnatural emphasis upon one single function of life. I admit, of course, its great but very variable importance. But the detection of transposed sexual elements in a variety of manifestations is not very practically useful, even if it is possible : and our experience is that the sexual components cannot even be correctly estimated except in relation to the individual style of life.

The erotic phases are functions of this individual life-style, and we can only gain insight into the erotic life, with all its waywardness, hesitation and elusive subtleties, so far as we can grasp the individual's style in the prototype. By the prototype I mean the original form of an individual's adaptation to life. The psychic prototype is a finished being by the time the child is four years old. (It is the baby in the man or woman, which never grows up any further, but rules the whole life to its end.) It is no wonder that certain religions have worshipped an infant, for this prototypic being is the greatest power in human life. The prototype is the constant factor, although we may improve its later manifestations to an indefinite extent when we come to recognise and understand it.

This prototype in each one is the baby Cupid who rules his behaviour as a lover. If the prototype is sociable and interested in others, the personality into whom it develops will solve all love-problems with loyalty to the partner and responsibility to society. If the prototype is struggling to attract notice and to suppress others, its later manifestation will include the use of sexuality towards the same ends : that person will establish sex-relationships in order to rule. A prototype formed by attaining superiority in a limited sphere of activity which excludes the opposite sex will tend later to produce homosexuality or other perversions. The main outlines of the erotic life are thus strictly pre-conditioned.

By the goal, therefore, especially in its most prototypic form, we can interpret the various sexual urges, while the converse does not hold good. The study of instincts or urges will never enable us to understand the structure of an individual psyche : and it is interesting to note that psychologists who endeavour to explain the mind's working from such observations instinctively presuppose a style of life without noticing that they have done so.

Love and marriage, from the standpoint of Individual Psychology, are the normal responses to the sexual question —one of the three vital questions of life—and our task is to understand the special difficulties they present to individuals. An individual who has been well prepared for social life in childhood will not have great difficulties in the sexual life. Courage, an optimistic attitude, common sense, and the feeling of being at home upon the crust of the earth, will enable him to face advantages and disadvantages with equal firmness. His goal of superiority will be identified with ideas of serving the human race and of overcoming its difficulties by his creative power. Deviations from the norm of sexual expression will be instinctively excluded as unattractive. His useful goal will so arrange all his emotions and actions that he will approach love in a feasible form ; whilst adolescent love-affairs and the experiences of his friends will train him for love and strengthen his position. The literature of unhappy love and disastrous marriage (a common source of mischief) will be unable to mislead him ; and even if he has disagreeable experiences with an unsuitable marriage-partner, it will not corrupt his course of life. His ideals of social life, of work and of beauty will survive ordinary defeats, and the sense of beauty itself be transferred to the beauty of adaptation to life.

Entirely different is the fate of those whose social contact is poor, who have lost real interest in the lives of others. They approach love without the right preparation—for every love-problem is a social problem in the sense that it is a question of behaviour towards another who is sexually attractive—and their unprepared souls feel as if the difficulty is insuperable when it comes to marriage, which is the most intimately and intensely social of all situations. Such a person has been educating himself for an isolated life, and does not really want to share life with another : so that he tends to shut his partner out from all but a few activities in which partnership seems necessary or advantageous. He does not conceive marriage as a complete human relationship. His difficulties are increased, very often, by having learnt about love and marriage from parents who were not happily united : and he gathers confirmation from his environment and from literature. In popular fiction the marriage situations are usually portrayed as unhappy ; unhappy love-stories are probably in a majority, because of the use which readers are making of them.

One of the chief obstacles to marriage lies in the prevailing opinion that the man is functionally superior, which leads men into vain expectations of rulership and makes girls rebel against their feminine function : they naturally reject a rôle of servitude in a " man-made world." Much suspicion, jealousy, and quarrelling springs directly from this antagonism, for if an individual feels victimised by love or marriage it disturbs every association of life. If a girl, for instance, feels that the feminine position is worse or lower than the masculine, she will enter into some sort of competition with the man in her striving to show superiority. If either of the partners is looking for a weaker mate in order to rule, disappointment is certain, for this is an expectant attitude : and it appears to be an immutable law of love and marriage that it can only succeed where the attitude is one of giving. When an individual's attitude towards love and marriage is hesitative, halting, or expectant, it indicates a general unpreparedness for social life, and we may safely infer a tendency to exclude a large part of the potentialities of life. In such cases the individual will always justify his actions, but his real purpose appears in the result, which is that love and marriage are indefinitely postponed. In this goal of evasion or exclusion, the means taken are interesting : they include all the neurotic symptoms which are more or less connected with sexual functions. The individual is like a stammerer in the sexual sphere. *Ejaculatio praecox*, lack of sex interest and satisfaction, vaginismus and frigidity, are all signs of a determination to exclude actions which the individual is apparently willing to perform.

Normally, of course, the sexual objective is in harmony with the life-goal, is indeed one aspect of it, and as soon as approach to this objective becomes possible it produces the thoughts and feelings which are appropriate, excluding all contradictions and conflicting tasks. But in the case of the neurotic, thoughts and feelings are produced which belong to other duties or functions of life ; irrelevant considerations are admitted which inhibit, traverse, or pervert normal conduct along the sexual line. The impotence or whatever sexual disability is thus produced is dictated by a neurotic goal of superiority and a mistaken style of life : and investigation always reveals a fixed intention to receive without giving, with a lack of social feeling, courage and optimistic activity.

There are other ways of excluding sexual partnership, of course, besides the functional disability. Exclusion is often contrived by an exaggerated and unpractical ideal of marriage : and sometimes by a desire to mate with persons obviously ineligible—much older, incurably diseased, or below the age of consent. When the patient has postponed marriage for a long period, perhaps attributing the indecision to polygamous tendencies, investigation will often disclose the under-structure of a perversion, which must not be mistaken for the motive, but recognised as a co-ordinate of the hesitative attitude.

A HUSBAND WHO DOMINATES THROUGH DRINKING

The efforts to exclude love and marriage, either before or after the contract, are modelled upon the prototypic or infantile pattern of adaptation, a fact which may be seen in the marriage-history of a young man who was twenty-three at the time when he first came to see me, without occupation and without friends. A year before this he had married a girl with whom he had relations for two years. His attitude towards her was one of continual jealousy, advice, and criticism. The girl appeared to be very docile while she was hoping to be married, and the man enjoyed a sense of superiority in this and in the knowledge that the marriage would antagonise his mother. After marriage, however, his wife was not so obedient, and he occasionally showed high temper. He behaved as he had behaved in childhood to his mother and his elder sister when they failed to gratify his wishes. Then he had screamed, run away from lessons, broken toys, torn his clothes, and in every possible way assailed his mother by attacks upon himself or his own occupations Now, after scenes with his wife, he would drink heavily and come home intoxicated.

This man was a spoiled child, who lost his father at the age of two years, and was pampered by the mother. He became the tyrant of the family, as children in such a position are likely to do : and from eight years old to thirteen he suffered from fainting-fits.

The connection between fainting and anger may in certain cases have an organic basis. I have found a type of patient who loses consciousness in a rage, and suspect some peculiarities in the blood-circulation of the brain. In such cases it is possible that an epileptoid fit occurs in varying degrees—petit mal, for example. If, as in this case, an outlet presents itself, there may be a discontinuance of the fits, and, as it happened, this patient was not obliged to repress his rages.

In accordance with the view of Individual Psychology, we should predict the repetition of this behaviour in childhood and expect the patient to take the same direction in any vital conflict with others—to hurt them by damaging himself. As such behaviour breeds callousness in the environment, the resentment and injury are correspondingly increased. In this case, when drunkenness ceased to punish the wife sufficiently, the man attempted suicide after a quarrel with her. He hurt himself severely and recovered very slowly. The inheritance of a large fortune from his father had lessened the patient's necessity for self-control. He could never keep a position in his occupation, a failure which he justified by complaining of terrible working conditions.

This case illustrates very well the inability of a pampered child to seize upon the best means to become a conqueror It also confirms the insufficiency of treating such conditions as drunkenness without recognition of the psychic prototype, for the latter can assimilate any change of conditions to its individual kind of striving. It is not interest in drink, but in himself and his own superiority that misleads such a patient towards the useless side of life. The object of treatment must be to quicken the social interest in whatever way is possible.

A WIFE WHO TAKES MORPHINE

The use of love and marriage as a means of domination is, of course, intolerable to the marriage partner ; so this man's wife gradually lost all interest in him. He obtained a divorce and married again twice. He took as his third wife a divorced woman who had attempted suicide during her first marriage, an attempt which she made when she was found out to have been unfaithful to her first husband because of his neglect of her. Her mother had been very critical and cold to her, failing in both of the two maternal functions : so that she had turned, as is usual, to the kinder father, and he had spoiled her with favour. This woman seemed to be of a very gentle disposition, but it did not stand the test of unfavourable situations. At school she had constantly made trouble in the class. She had only one friend, and was not sociable.

Her second husband was a youngest child, left-handed, and with a clumsiness which drew upon him the constant derision of his elder brothers. He was, however, very ambitious and anxious to surpass the brothers, who in childhood had beaten him by his handicap, and this stimulated him to the conquest of wealth : he became rich and highly esteemed. Fear of defeat and escape from derision made up his prototype, so that he liked and sought isolation. His first two marriages were brought about by women who flattered him. The second of them had appeared when he had lost a great part of his fortune—the money which, to him, stood for superiority over his brothers. This woman had tried to console him with morphia, which he continued to take after she died.

The third wife, described above, married him with a determination to save him from the drug habit, and her first efforts revealed her inability to do so. Like the spoilt child she was, she was infuriated at her lack of power over him, and began taking to morphia herself in order to punish him. She had the idea that he would reform himself if he saw the terrible consequences of his action ; but as nothing of the kind happened, both continued the abuse of the drug, and soon each of them noticed that the other was looking about for another partner.

This couple tried several morphia cures without success, which is not surprising when we review the complex of motives at work. One was the man's childish goal of superiority, to escape derision or disesteem. Another lay in his attitude to his business worries, from which he not only found partial relief in morphia, but also a subjectively valid excuse. His diminished success could be blamed upon the morphia, without which, he could still believe, he would have triumphed over everything. He sometimes spoke of the habit in both ways, as a relief and as an excuse, without understanding the connection or the contradiction between them.   To do this he would have had to relate these manifestations to his style of life, to understand his exaggerated demand for esteem, in which case he might have taken better means to attain it. His polygamous tendencies, and his exclusion of friends, showed a lack of social adjustment : and he could not possibly have been cured by taking away the morphia. It was the whole personality which needed to be changed, by the recognition of its prototype. It is true, that, in lighter cases, a patient with very varied symptoms may lose them before he himself or the doctor have come to grasp their coherence. When this happens it is either because of a favourable change in the patient's situation or because the doctor, by encouragement or by chance, renews the patient's interest in others.

The wife was far from being cured of the drug. Feeling in danger of losing her second husband she gave up attempts to cure him, and being indifferent to the criticism of others, and if anything courting the displeasure of her mother, she increased her own doses of morphia to the most dangerous excesses. This was a repetition of her conduct in her first marriage where she was neglected. This drug habit was a kind of suicide. Being a youngest child and the father's favourite, both her desire for conquest and her feeling of inadequacy were intense : and she lived according to the neurotic formula—" All or nothing." In these cases, when the hope of gaining *all* begins to fade, *nothing* is left ; and this must be expressed by very bad habits, suicide or insanity. The feeling that suicide gives mastery over life and death is the supreme expression of the goal of superiority on the useless side of life. But we must note, of course, that the patient began to be watched with apprehension by her father and husband. Everybody became more tender towards her : giving her a sense of augmented power and importance.

— — — — — —

Such are the underlying difficulties which obstruct so many attempts to cure drunkenness, drug-habits, and suicidal tendencies. There is a method for everything in life : and to solve any problem we must find the right one. There are two ways, for instance, of trying to pass through a doorway only five feet high. One of them is to walk erect, and the other is to bend one's back. If I try the first method I not only bump my head on the lintel but have to fall back upon the second method after all. I call this the law of the low doorway. Nothing compels me to stoop, but if I do not realise the relation between my height and the aperture I cannot possibly pass through it. We stand in an equally definite relation to the critical personal problems of life. If we do not realise the fact and adapt our method accordingly we come into collision with reality.

Every child is confronted with reality, and finds its method, more or less successfully, in its prototype. These individual responses to reality are so wonderfully varied that the ancient poets and fable-writers compared them with species of animals such as the hare, the fox, the stork, and the snake. Prototypes are indeed like animal souls, moving each towards its own goal, in its own interest and its own characteristic manner.

The tension between the child and its environment—which is never entirely absent—is never exactly calculable, for besides the many possibilities of variation in the family constellation, each child has its individual sensitiveness and an original responsiveness. Thus, against a fairly typical position of inferiority, different children will erect most diverse concrete goals of superiority. There are many children, for example, who are at a similar disadvantage through weak muscles and poor eyesight, but they may compensate in directions which will lead them to be acrobats or artists or towards a hundred other developments, according to the originality of their reaction, the degree of their courage, and their social feeling. Moreover, the defects which they have to compensate are full of subtle individual differences.

It is for this reason that a child which has deviated from a normal line of life cannot be re-educated by normal methods. The method must be specially adapted : for the child with an abnormal endowment or development will feel suppressed in perfectly normal situations. A child with stomach trouble, for example, may fail to gain in weight, and develop poorly : and if the circumstances are not carefully adapted the usual consequences will ensue— a pessimistic and hostile attitude, perhaps with pugnacity and irritability. Such a child is liable to contract an envious disposition by comparing itself with others : it may show an abnormal interest in eating and eatables, and its tendency to collect and hoard things may develop in later life into a concentration upon money-making. It is common to find troubles in early nutrition in families which produce successful money-makers. As a rule, when a child displays exaggerated consciousness of its stomach and a tendency to anxiety, we should do something about it, for it is a common beginning of neurosis. There is a feeling of curtailment and a loss of interest in others, which bode ill for the child's future.

Children with stomach troubles are a well-known source of trouble to parents and physicians, but the difficulties are due far more to imperfect methods than to the constitutional deficiency. This is the case with other physical disabilities : the better we understand their connection with the general line of life the better the methods we can devise. We cannot claim that we have found the universally perfect method, but the continued search for right methods according to the principles of Individual Psychology certainly enables us to avoid many mistakes.

THE MISTRESS WITH HEADACHES AND PALPITATIONS

The dominance of the prototypic attitude in love and marriage is exemplified in the following case. As a girl, the patient was the second child of the family, very weak, very pretty, spoiled by her mother and ill-used by a drunken father She lost the mother's favouritism at the age of three, when a baby sister was born, and protested by becoming truculent and high-tempered. She was supposed to inherit bad temper from her father, and some psychologists would uphold this mistaken opinion, but any child might take this line of development in such an unfavourable turn of circumstances. Indeed, from the attitudes of aggressive, disobedient, or domineering children we are often able to guess correctly at some salient feature of the home environment, such as this displacement by a younger child.

This girl became an actress and had many love-affairs, which culminated in her becoming the mistress of an elderly man. Such an obvious exploitation of advantage indicates deep feelings of insecurity and cowardice. This relationship, however, brought her trouble : her mother reproached her, and although the man loved her he could not get a divorce. During this time her younger sister became engaged.

In the face of this competition, she began to suffer from headaches and palpitation, and became very irritable towards the man. This was a neurotic impatience, and it was the cause of her coming to consult me. In a certain type we find that headaches are regularly produced by severe tensions of anger. The emotion accumulates so to speak during a period in which the patient shows no symptoms. The emotional tension may actually result in circulatory changes producing attacks of trigeminal neuralgia, migraine and epileptiform seizures. An illustration of such circulatory disturbances is provided by the well-known respiratory spasms and sensations of choking induced by violent rage.

In those cases of trigeminal neuralgia which have no organic basis I have already emphasised (1910) the importance of psychological factors   These may, of course, act through vascular disturbances induced by emotion, and the frequent repetition of such interferences with the blood supply may in the end cause organic damage to the tissues of the nervous system.

The tendency to anger is related to excessive ambition : both of which originate in a competitive striving to escape from a sense of being overcome. They occur in unsocial natures, who feel uncertain of attaining their goal by patient striving, and often try to escape to the useless side upon an outburst of temper. Children make use of such explosions to conquer by terrifying, or at least to feel superior : and in a similar way they use the consequences— their headaches. The neurotic origin of headaches was not known to the scientific world when I first spoke of it in 1910, but it must have been well known in antiquity. Horace, in an ode to Mæcenas, wrote of those ambitious persons who do not want to alter themselves but only to change others ; and he refers to their headaches and sleeplessness.

To return to the case : the girl's condition was the result of a neurotic method of striving to hasten her marriage, and was not at all ineffective. The married man was greatly worried by her continuous headaches, and made efforts to get a divorce, but he was not very courageous, and made slow progress against the opposition to it. The girl then broke with him and wanted to marry another man ; but she soon discovered he was too uncultured, so she returned to her former lover. He (the married man), then came to see me about my patient, and said that he would hurry on the divorce and marry her.

Treatment of the *immediate* illness was easy—in fact, it would have cleared up without me, for the girl was powerful enough to succeed with the help of her headaches. Her goal was to force the man to get a divorce quickly ; it was the goal of her childhood, not to be surpassed by her younger sister : and as soon as the divorce proceedings began the headaches disappeared.

I explained to her the connection between her headaches and the competitive attitude to her sister. She felt incapable of attaining her goal of superiority by normal means, for she was one of those children whose interest has become absorbed in themselves, and who tremble for fear that they will not succeed. She admitted that she only cared for herself and did not like the man she was about to marry.

Her palpitation was due to the fact that she had twice been pregnant and both times had resorted to abortion, when she justified herself to the doctor by saying that her heart was too weak for her to bear children. It was true that her heart was irritated by tense situations and suppressed anger, but she used this symptom increasingly and exaggerated it to justify her intention never to have children. Self-absorbed women generally show their lack of human and social interest by an unwillingness to have children : but sometimes, of course, they desire children for reasons of ambition or for fear of being considered inferior.

A dream of this patient is worth recording. She dreamed that she was well dressed and held a naked baby in her arms. She said to the baby, which was of a brown and jolly complexion, " I cannot take care of you, I must give you up." The baby answered, " Yes, you are right." Then she began crying in her dream, and a man passed her, but she turned her head to avoid being seen. The man, however, wished to see her and looked at her.

By the nakedness of the baby she meant that she was too poor to have children. Her sister was to be married to a rich man, whereas she had only enough money for her own clothes, none to spare for a child. The baby's brown complexion meant that she could have a healthy child, but the dream-child reassured her, by agreeing with her, that everyone could see it was impossible for her to have children. The patient said at this time that she felt perfectly well, but suffered from palpitation of the heart night and morning, which showed she was clinging to the idea that her weak heart would excuse her from having children. She was too egoistical and much too eager to keep in the centre of the stage of life, to entertain the prospect of children, and moreover she felt the child as a potential rival, because the tragedy of her infantile life was one of rivalry with her baby sister. The man who passed by her in the dream must have been myself, and her turning away was a sign that she did not wish to be entirely open with me : she was afraid that I would blame her, and as she knew I wished to develop her social feeling she thought I should wish her to have a child.

The decision whether a woman should or should not have a child, should rest entirely with the woman—such at least is my personal belief. I cannot see the use of forcing a child upon a woman who is without social interest or love for children : for she is almost certain to bring it up badly. In such cases I prefer to adjust the woman socially, and then, I am sure she will wish to have a baby without suggestion or pressure from anyone else.

———————

It is, or used to be, the almost invariable conclusion of Freudian psychologists, that the person who excludes love is repressing his libido, but it is a vast improvement both in diagnosis and treatment when we relate this exclusion to the individual's goal of superiority. If the exclusion of normal possibilities of mating is very persistent and obstinate it is always a sign that the person is neurotic in other relations also, and does not want to see marriage in the obvious light of social necessity because of a more general exclusion of social behaviour. We then see a hesitating or evasive attitude before the love-problem, or an unnatural tendency in the love-relation, both of which proceed from a mistake in understanding the relation between the individual's prototypic needs and the possibilities of his situation. A better understanding would produce better behaviour. For individual goals are not unattainable, nor are they attainable in one way only, but every way of attainment has its own sequence of necessary obligations. The neurotic is paying the price of taking the most difficult, lonely, and impracticable way to the summit of his ambitions, when there are much easier and better paths. In a sense it may be said that the prototype never relinquishes his rule over the individual's life, but there are better and better ways of fulfilling its law.

We must regard the love-problem as the most intimate and organically-determined form of the problem of social behaviour, a view which acts as a continual corrective of mistakes. This view of Individual Psychology may not bless us with an absolute truth ; it may not enable us to foresee the future of a marriage as accurately as we can calculate the path of a falling stone. But the stone lies in a world of truth, whereas we live in the realm of human mistakes. Our method enables us to replace the great mistakes by small ones, and that is our justification for believing that we can often help others to approach their own goals with a method which, if perhaps not infallible, is better than theirs in social direction. In the world of the psyche there is no principle of individual orientation beyond our own beliefs. Very great are the consequences of our real beliefs. Big mistakes can produce neuroses but little mistakes a nearly normal person.

V

Neurotic Life Style and Psychotherapy

IT is natural for an individual to express himself with his whole body, so that it is often more instructive to watch a person's movements—how he walks, sits, smiles or fidgets —than to hear what he says. We may go further, and apply this to the valuation of symptoms. Vomiting, for example, is commonly a sign that the person who vomits does not wish to agree. It is an attack upon another, or the rejection of an approach. Fainting may also be the effective rejection of a situation in which a person feels entirely powerless.

How could I cure a stutterer if I believed stuttering to be caused by some subtle and unknown organic deficiencies ? I have plenty of evidence that the stutterer does not want to join with others, and he can generally talk quite well when he is alone : he may even be able to read or recite excellently : so that I can only inter- pret his stammer as the expression of his attitude towards others.

There is some point, however, in the belief, common in America, that stuttering is caused by training left-handed children to use the right hand, although this is only because wrong methods are used, which give the child an anti-social bias in reaction to unsympathetic criticism   A mechanical and competitive method of teaching makes no proper allowance for the fact that the left-handed child has more actual difficulty in adapting itself, and the child retaliates with an impediment which worries or irritates its teachers.   There is no physical reason why children should not be taught to use the right hand.   Since we are living in a right-handed culture, left-handedness may sometimes be felt as if it were an inferiority in later periods of life.   In many technical and commercial positions and even in social life left-handedness may be a noticeable disability or hindrance.   But the training of these people for a right-handed world should be done with the correct method, for they are a large minority whose rights should be protected.   In early life the left-handed child has certainly greater difficulties, for often the peculiarity is not recognised, and blame is incurred for clumsiness.   Such a child connects its imperfect dexterity with all other difficulties at home and at school, and suffers from a depression which centres its interest too much in itself.   Thus left-handed children often acquire the feeling that the world is a dangerous place, and become more liable to neurosis than others.

I believe about thirty-five per cent. of all persons are left-handed, and most of them unconscious of the fact.   There are several ways of detecting the left-handed : the best-known and simplest is to ask the person in question to clasp his hands together ; the left-handed subject will instinctively do this so that the left thumb is over the right thumb. The eyebrow on the left side is frequently higher in a left-handed person, and the whole symmetry of the body more developed on the left side. Even in the cradle we can see when a baby tends to use the left side of the body more than the right. The adaptation to right-handedness is a somewhat severe test for these children. Generally, when I see a very bad handwriting I know it is that of a left-handed person whose courage is below par. On the other hand, if I see excellent handwriting I know it is a left-handed person also, but one who has successfully grappled with his difficulties. The left-handed who develop their right hands tend to some artistic or craftsmanlike powers. Among painters we find not a few left-handed persons who paint equally well with either hand.

It is not generally known that left-handed children very often have considerable difficulty in learning to read because they spell reversely from right to left ; a mistake which they can correct if it is properly explained to them.[1]

Imperfections in the sense-organs limit the means which a child has of sharing in the life of others. They impose necessary differences of behaviour which may be felt as a burden if we do not meet the case with wise measures of encouragement. Children with imperfect sight walk cautiously, as they are conscious of danger in movement. They are more interested in seeing because it is difficult for them, and if they compensate well they will become visual

[1] These and other facts have been collected and discussed by Dr. Alice Friedmann in an article entitled, "Fragebogen für Untersuchung auf Linkshändigkeit" ("Questionnaire for the investigation of left-handedness") (*Int. Z. Indiv. Psychol.*, 1927, 5, 193–196).

types. There are corresponding compensations for poor hearing and for handicaps in movement.

Gustav Freytag, for example, was very short-sighted and did not wear glasses. Not being able to see much, his attention was focussed upon imagining what his environment was like, and the high development of his fancy was his great quality as a writer. Goethe, Schiller, Milton, and many other fine poets were afflicted with poor sight, and also many of the greatest painters. A child with perfectly normal sight is not likely to concentrate his attention upon the phenomena of visibility but takes them for granted. It must never be assumed, however, that defective visual powers will be necessarily compensated with talent or brilliance, or indeed in any socially useful way. A good compensation will only be made where there is courage and a favourable situation : then we may count upon a special development, either relative to the same sense function, or to another, such as hearing. If the situation is unfavourable and courage fails, there will be a negative compensation —*e.g.*, the child will not *want* to see anything.

Those whose eyes are normal sometimes develop interests which depend upon visual powers, but not unless they have at some time been confronted with the necessity to see. No advance is ever made without the consciousness of a hindrance. It is the thing which appears to be a deterrent which acts as the incentive whenever there is a courageous struggle for success. I have already referred to the aural difficulties of Beethoven, Smetana, Dvorak, and other musicians.

Our civilisation is not only a right-handed but also a masculine one : so that the striving for superiority tends to

elaborate an over-masculine attitude. Several great philosophers have remarked this, as Kant did when he said "No man
ever wants to be a woman." I do not entirely agree with this,
for I have known cases in which men wished to be women. A
bow-legged man, for instance, told me he wished he were a
woman with skirts to cover his unshapely legs, and there are
spoiled boys who would like to be women in order to be petted.

I should never oppose women for taking their place in the
world upon an equal footing with men, but I have seen that
it is better to bring up boys and girls from the earliest age
to be reconciled with their respective social rôles. When
a girl believes that she may change into a boy it is because
the female rôle has not been presented to her in an aspect
of equality. She rebels against what she feels to be a
prospect of permanent inferiority. The Freudians have
interpreted this fact as the so-called "castration complex,"
because girls frequently have the fantasy that the male
organs have been surgically removed from them : but this
is to mistake the effect for the cause. Almost every girl
wishes at times to be a boy, even when she says that she
prefers to be a woman, because the masculine position
appears to be safer. She shows that she has weighed up the
advantages and disadvantages of both. In Herder's
collection of songs of brides, we cannot help being struck by
the fact that they are all sad songs ; showing the girl's
apprehension that she will not be appreciated or esteemed
in marriage. In the crisis between girlhood and woman-
hood she fears the loss of virginity as if it were the loss of
potentiality or dignity. It is this feeling which accounts
for various manifestations in women, such as a suspicious attitude, desire to escape from love and marriage,
vaginismus, shyness before pregnancy, and also perversions.

Girls often want to dress as boys, to play like boys, and even to be called by boys' names. I was once walking with a five-year-old girl, and she led me to a store with boys' clothing displayed in the window. She asked me to buy her a boy's suit. I resorted to artfulness and said, yes, I would buy it for her if she wanted it, but *no boy* would want to wear a girl's dress. She was silent for a while and then pointed to a boy's overcoat and said : " Please, won't you at least buy me that coat."

In such a child we may infer that at the age of two or three there had been uncertainty of the unchangeable nature of the sexual rôle, and this uncertainty had influenced the formation of the psychic prototype. If a girl is stimulated to imitate boys by her environment or her education it will increase her difficulties later when she has to face her problem as a human being. Girls should be educated, not as if for a lower function, but with a view and a sense of their special social responsibilities and possibilities. Without this preparation, girls are likely to show the need of it later, especially in adolescence, when they first enter into a little freedom and independence ; then they often like to exaggerate masculine ways and manners, and especially to imitate the bad ones, such as drinking and sexual liberties. At the present time, the masculine protest is rampant and widely displayed by women of all ages, who smoke, wear short skirts and short hair and do everything possible to approximate to masculine manners.

THE BOY WHO THOUGHT HE WAS A PROPHET

A boy of fifteen years old was brought to me from a sanatorium, after having been treated by many physicians for having made unaccountable motions with his hands, contortions of facial expression and abnormalities of speech : he often screamed without any apparent reason. His symptoms resembled schizophrenia, but eventually he told me his secret. " I know it is rubbish," he said, " but I believe I am a prophet. No one must know it." In a few days I was able to cure him. He did not wish to associate with others, and he was isolating himself by his extraordinary behaviour. He had a younger sister, which is always a difficult position for the older boy. Although his school record was a good one—in fact, he was the best pupil in the school—his determination to play a unique part in life had brought him into universal dislike. His flight into the world of unreality, where alone he could feel a sufficient degree of superiority, was only caused by cowardice. Finally it had become necessary for him to speak a different language from the others, and to regard all his schoolmates together as one victorious and foreign nation, for they had teased and beaten him ! Meanwhile at home he felt more and more that his sister was advancing and that for the second time he would lose his superiority, and this upset him altogether. He had no courage to tell his parents that he felt suppressed, and at school he escaped into fancy. In his dream-world, therefore, he made himself a prophet. The singular contortions and grimaces which he had begun to use were modelled upon gestures which he had originally invented to attract his parents' attention to himself.

He was able to take an optimistic line with me, because he felt able to reveal *to me only* the secret of his greatness. On the basis of this mutual confidence he could discuss and reconsider his relations with others, and with the help of my explanation and encouragement he recovered the natural desire to adapt himself to life. I have had similar cases, in which spoiled children have suffered much from the cruelty of their comrades.

Another case in which neurosis was involved with a prophetic rôle was that of a merchant, forty years old, who came to me for help because he found himself unable to speak to people. In social surroundings he was overcome by a tension like stage-fright ; he trembled, was abashed, and felt a sensation of choking. He had married a widow twelve years his senior, who spoiled him very much as his mother had done before. With her and with a very few intimate friends, as well as with his customers, he could converse without any difficulty, but his behaviour could not stand the test of any wider circle of society.

I could not find the clue to this strange situation until the man mentioned that he had prophetic dreams. Then I suspected at once that his goal of superiority was to be a prophet, in a privileged and unique relationship with God. I cautiously hinted at this idea to him, beginning with a " perhaps," and he at once replied, " All my friends know that I am a clairvoyant, and so does my wife. Many cases have proved it." This, of course, was the cause of his difficulty. If he spoke freely in society he would be in danger of betraying some error in his knowledge, which might ruin his fame as a clairvoyant. In the tension of facing this possibility of defeat he choked, and his clairvoyance was thus defended by a mysterious speechlessness.

THE CLAIRVOYANT AND SPEECHLESS MERCHANT

In the first interviews with a patient we have to make sure whether the case is really one of neurosis. My own practice, after hearing the patient's complaints, is to proceed in one of two ways. If I suspect that there is no real organic derangement, I may temporarily exclude that aspect of the case from consideration, and proceed to investigate the circumstances and style of life. If, on the other hand, there is evident organic disturbance, I consider whether the complaint and suffering is greater than the illness itself would justify, *i.e.*, whether there is present a combination of organic and psychic illness. I have often found more pain than the illness warrants, for instance, and also unaccountable excitement accompanying an injurious illness, which may increase the course of the fever. In organic illness also the appetite varies according to the general outlook, and a serious illness may be prolonged or even fatally influenced if the patient turns pessimistic or becomes psychically lethargic.

In these cases the most urgent need is to find out whether the patient is confronted with a problem which he feels unable to solve. Hardly ever, of course, can we get at this directly. If possible, I discuss the course of the patient's life with him from earliest childhood, noting especially the incidents or phases which reveal or conceal the most painful sense of weakness and impotence : and at the same time I keep myself alert to the signs of organic inferiority. Wherever we can surely detect a disposition to hesitate, halt, or escape, we have a clue to the present position also. When the illness proves to be both organic and psychic the treatment must proceed upon both lines at the same time. If the disturbance is dominantly or entirely of a psychic nature, I explain to the patient what I have discovered from the first conversation, but in such a way that it cannot be discouraging, and taking the greatest care not to tell the patient anything he is not yet able to understand.

To verify my findings, I check one indication by another, eliciting information of most various kinds. I ask, for instance, "What would you do if I cured you immediately?" a question which I may expect will draw a reference to some present problem not hitherto discussed. I ask for the patient's earliest remembrance to get a hint as to the dominant interest in life. I try to understand what is happening by noting what activities, of a kind normally to be expected, are being excluded by the patient. At the same time I am careful to ask myself if I should have been of the same type as I think I have before me if I were in the same circumstances and following the same style of life. As soon as I feel I have grasped his circumstances, I enquire whether the patient's thoughts, feelings, actions, and characteristics are all working in the same direction, towards the exclusion or at least the postponement of the present problem. The accumulated experiences of Individual Psychologists justify us in looking for this unity in the life-plan, and a wide knowledge of the literature and working tradition of Individual Psychology is of great value in diagnosis, as it helps us to identify the typical neurotic factors, such as the lack of social interest, failure in courage and self-confidence, and rejection of common sense. We can thus more easily comprehend the style of life : and if we always check and verify each impression by others, we shall not be misled into mere generalisations.

The discussion invariably reveals an accented " if." " I would marry *if* " ; " I would resume my work *if* " ; or " I would sit for my examination *if* " ; and so on. The neurotic has always collected some more or less plausible reasons to justify his escape from the challenge of life, but he does not realise what he is doing. The patient must be led very carefully, and it is the duty of the psychologist to train his patient in the faculty of simple and direct explanation.

The psycho-therapist must lose all thought of himself and all sensitiveness about his ascendancy, and must never demand anything of the patient. His is a belated assumption of the maternal function, and he must work with a corresponding devotion to the patient's needs. What the Freudians call transference (so far as we can discuss it apart from sexual implications) is merely social feeling. The patient's social feeling, which is always present in some degree, finds its best possible expression in the relation with the psychologist. The so-called " resistance " is only lack of courage to return to the useful side of life : which causes the patient to put up a defence against treatment, for fear that his relation with the psychologist should force him into some useful activity in which he will be defeated. For this reason we must never force a patient, but guide him very gently towards his easiest approach to usefulness. If we apply force he is certain to escape. My own practice, also, is never to advise marriage or free relations. I find it always leads to bad results. A person who is told that he should marry or seek sexual experience is quite likely to develop impotence. The first rule in treatment is to win the patient ; the second is for the psychologist never to worry about his own success : if he does so he forfeits it.

The elimination of all constraint, the freest possible relationship—these are the indispensable conditions between patient and physician. For a cure depends upon their unity in understanding the patient's goal which has been hitherto a heavily-guarded secret. I have already alluded to this necessity for the truth underlying the individual life-style in reference to the treatment of drunkenness, morphia-taking, and similar habits. Merely to take away the poison and say some encouraging words is useless. The patient must realise *why* he took to drink. Insufficient also would be his recognition of the general principles of Individual Psychology, that those who turn inebriate have lost social courage and interest, or succumbed to fear of an imminent defeat. It is easy for the physician to say, and even for the patient to believe, that he turned to drink because of a sense of inferiority which originated in childhood, but nothing will come out of the mere phraseology. The physician must grasp the special structure and development of that individual life with such accuracy, and express it with such lucidity, that the patient knows he is plainly understood and recognises his own mistake. When patients or practitioners come to me and say : " We have explained everything," or " We quite understand, and yet we cannot succeed," I consider their statements ridiculous. Always if I go into such a case of failure I find that neither physician nor patient have understood the matter nor explained anything. Sometimes the patient has felt inferior and suppressed by the physician, and resisted all true explanation. Occasionally the tables have been turned and the patient has been treating the doctor ! Not infrequently an inexperienced practitioner teaches the patient the theories of Individual Psychology, in such phrases as " You lack social courage, you are not interested in others, you feel inferior," and so forth, which may be worse than useless. A real explanation must be so clear that the patient knows and feels his own experience in it instantly.

ESCAPE THROUGH DRINKING

I treated a case of drunkenness in a man thirty-two years of age, very intelligent, well-educated and perfectly healthy, who had regular bouts of drinking at intervals of four weeks. He had had many treatments and remedies, including injections of the extracts of various glands. He had spent months in the lock-up, but nothing had changed his habits.

The man was very shy, trembled and smoked cigarettes incessantly. This behaviour confirmed the impression I had formed at the first glance, that he felt me as a superior and an enemy : and he clung to his cigarette, not to be submerged by his feeling of comparative worthlessness. In answer to my questions he said he had no friends and did not go into society, had no occupation, and was not in love. He preferred to remain alone, and if he was urged to join in any social gathering he became highly excited. He lived extravagantly at the expense of his parents, paying the highest prices for more or less useless things whenever he chose to do so. We can guess his answer to the sexual problem : it was masturbation, which is the style of sexual life adapted to confirm isolation and to avoid love and marriage.

Such a way of living usually originates in the prototypic attitude of a pampered child, who feels obliged to keep out of the firing-line of life because he is not prepared for it. This man made his escape by being a drunkard. When he came to face the problems of society, work, and love, unsupported by others, strained situations and tense attitudes were his intermittent and periodical experiences, so that uncontrollable bouts of drunkenness were an appropriate solution of his problem on the useless side of life.

The usual tensions of every day were not severe enough to drive him to drink, and he was able to use his sober intervals to display good intentions of giving up the habit altogether. He did not strive to make his environment hopeless, as the fighting type of child often does, but was able to continue in his own line of error by means of these intervals of remorse and repentance, which always induced others to give him another chance and to hope that " this time really was the last." The drunkenness would begin sometimes when he was expected to go into society, and sometimes when actually in company with others or at a party. It appeared when there was a demand of duty, or if he met a girl who regarded him as a possible husband ; and when he was short of money and his parents did not wire a remittance to him quickly enough, he also resorted immediately to drink. He was partly conscious of the use he was making of his indulgence, but he never understood its general tendency as an escape, nor that he was always ready to compromise himself and make himself impossible.

His evident aim was to be relieved of every duty and to be supported for his own sake alone. Self-centred and wholly lacking social adjustment, he had nevertheless attained a goal of superiority by the elimination of defeat. He had no defeat in society for he did not enter it ; no defeat in work, for he had no occupation ; no defeat in love—he avoided it. Subjectively, he triumphed over life, lived it upon his own terms entirely : but objectively, of course, the terms he obtained were almost the worst possible.

He proved to have been a spoilt child, who wanted to face every situation by means of parental support. He was an only boy among three sisters. He was carefully educated and succeeded at school because the teachers were persuaded by the parents to pamper him. When he grew out of his sheltered years life looked impossible to him, so he made his escape. This patient's father used to drink, and he knew from an early age how this habit worried his mother and occupied her thoughts with the father. One day before a school examination he got drunk for the first time. His mother was much worried, believing that this was a hereditary taint in his disposition, and took greater care of him in the hope of curing him. Not to lose this success, the patient continued to drink.

This man's earliest memory referred to a time when his parents were away, and he was left to the care of his grandmother. He did not feel well during this period. Once, when his grandmother criticised him, he packed up some of his belongings and ran away, and the grandmother had to follow him. He was four years old at the time, and this recollection indicates his prototypic attitude to life. Whenever he did not feel spoilt he escaped into drunkenness. All neurotic persons who have developed from a pampered prototype expect to be appreciated *before* they will do anything of social value instead of *after* having done it, thus expecting the natural course of things to be reversed in their own favour.

This patient had to be trained to feel at home in the wider environment of the world, and encouraged until he could afford to recognise its real and necessary demands. This, as I have said before, involves the assumption by the psychologist of the two maternal functions : first, winning the patient's trust as a fellow-man, and then, directing this new confidence towards other persons and towards the advantages and disadvantages of real life : his mother had failed in the second function and it had devolved upon me.

In the beginning of the treatment there was a possibility that he might hurt himself or others with a more desperate escape into intoxication than ever, and steps had to be taken to watch him. No rule can be given how best to do this, but whatever is done must be arranged with the agreement of the patient. Otherwise the patient would fight the physician in the same way that he fought the parents, by exploiting his own weakness—the drunkenness. If it is necessary to keep him under supervision against his will—in an asylum, for instance—let someone else place him there. The physician must in no way interfere with him, and then he will not be hindered by his antagonism.

———

In relation to Nature as a whole, man is in an inferior position, so that he is obliged to develop on the side of strategy and trickery. In our over-intellectualised civilisation especially, practically everyone is wonderfully adept in the use of his own individual tricks : the really important differences of conduct are not those of individual cleverness but of usefulness or uselessness. By useful I mean in the interests of mankind generally. The most sensible estimate of the value of any activity is its helpfulness to all mankind, present and future, a criterion that applies not only to that which subserves the immediate preservation of life, but also to higher activities such as religion, science, and art. It is true that we cannot always decide what is strictly worth while from this point of view. But we know when we are guided by the impulse to act usefully, and the better a person's social adjustment is, the nearer he approaches to true perception. A person who is on the path of self-isolation and withdrawal may perhaps get to know or acquire valuable potentialities, but even then society does not benefit by these new possibilities until they are realised through the socially directed activity of himself or of others.

Whether a given line of life is really due to a social or an a-social impulse is shown by contact with reality. A life may develop remarkably well or ill, perhaps at a late stage, and people are astonished by it, and try to explain it by chance, by inherited tendencies, or by destiny, when it is really due to the inherent social or anti-social feeling in the goal of the individual. And the a-social tendencies and mistakes which we can trace in the early life of a child are also to be seen in the behaviour of a whole family or in the thought of a nation. The only way in which we can hope to avoid these mistakes is by learning to increase our social feeling, which alone can save us from worthless and injurious activities.

It is almost impossible to exaggerate the value of an increase in social feeling. The mind improves, for intelligence is a communal function. The feeling of worth and value is heightened, giving courage and an optimistic view, and there is a sense of acquiescence in the common advantages and drawbacks of our lot. The individual feels at home in life and feels his existence to be worth while just so far as he is useful to others and is overcoming common instead of private feelings of inferiority. Not only the ethical nature, but the right attitude in æsthetics, the best understanding of the beautiful and the ugly will always be founded upon the truest social feeling.

Whilst the child is wholly embedded in the family group it is not easy to be sure whether it is developing social feeling and useful interest : this only appears with certainty when the first new situation is encountered. This is generally the arrival of a baby brother or sister, or the entrance into kindergarten or school. In one or another of these situations the child either passes or fails in his first examination in fitness for life. A child who refuses to go to school, does not pay attention when it is there, works badly or will not associate with its schoolfellows, shows the inadequacy of its preparation. If allowed to develop such a plan of life it may very probably be unable to take its place in society.

Neurosis invariably gives relief to the subject, not, of course, in the light of objectivity and common sense, but according to his own private logic : it secures some triumph or at least it allays the fear of defeat. Thus neurosis is the weapon of the coward, and the weapon most used by the weak. We cannot ignore the heavily-veiled aggressive or vindictive element in most neuroses.

SUICIDAL TENDENCIES IN A MEDICAL STUDENT

I had a case of a medical student who wanted to commit suicide, an undersized man, who consequently wanted to be tall. He was very much spoiled by his mother, who was the wife of a physician, a tyrannical husband with whom she was not happy. One day the cook came into the room screaming and crying out that the father had made a sexual assault upon her. From this time the mother went into depression and cried continually. The boy could not understand this, and wanted me to explain it to him. He had already asked his mother how she could be so much depressed by the unfaithfulness of a husband for whom she neither had nor professed any affection : but she interrupted his question by screaming, " You cannot possibly understand this ! " The student said, in answer to my enquiry whether the father's behaviour was as brutal or rough as before, that on the contrary he was very quiet, calm, and considerate.

" Do you think ? " I then asked, " that your mother will give up her only means of taming this tyrant ? She pays the price with her depression, but she feels that she is the conqueror. You are doing something very similar. You used to be your mother's favourite, but now you are alone in a foreign city, deprived of the attentions of your mother, who is so busy taming your father. You are failing in your work at the university, and are not prepared to be independent, so you wish to impress your mother with your suicidal impulses just as your mother impresses your father with her depression. You have been trained, as pampered children often are, to succeed by a display of weakness."

———————

In the investigation of a neurotic style of life we must always suspect an opponent, and note who suffers most because of the patient's condition. Usually this is a member of the family, and sometimes a person of the other sex, though there are cases in which the illness is an attack upon society as a whole. There is always this element of concealed accusation in neurosis, the patient feeling as though he were deprived of his *right*—*i.e.*, of the centre of attention —and wanting to fix the responsibility and blame upon someone. By such hidden vengeance and accusation, by excluding social activity whilst fighting against persons and rules, the problem-child and the neurotic find some relief from their dissatisfaction. There are cases in which the revenge-motive is fairly obvious, as it was with a neurotic woman I treated whose marriage was entirely unhappy, and yet she would never divorce her husband, preferring to remain a continual accusation against him. It must be remembered, however, that neurotics generally, like perverts, drunkards, and morphia-maniacs, have not wholly denied their social feeling, which still keeps them from crime and suicide.

VI

Neurotic Use of Emotions

BECOMING DEPRESSED WHEN ALL IS WELL

A CURIOUS case of depression which I once treated illustrates very clearly how sadness may be used to heighten the feeling of superiority. This was the case of a man of fifty, who said he felt perfectly healthy except when he was in a notably comfortable situation. It was when he was at a concert or theatre with his family, for instance, that a fit of melancholy would descend upon him : and in such depression he always remembered an intimate friend who had died when he was twenty-five. This friend had been his rival, not only in business but as a suitor for the hand of his wife— an unsuccessful rival, however, for by the time he contracted his fatal illness, my patient already had the advantage over him both in love and in business.

Success had been his lot, both before and after the friend's death ; he was the favourite of his parents, unsurpassed by brothers and sisters, and prosperous in the world. His wife, however, was an ambitious character who strove to solve every domestic problem by a personal triumph or conquest, moral or otherwise : and between two such persons, the struggle was naturally continuous and severe. The wife sometimes gained the ascendancy very cleverly, not by quarrelling or domineering in any way, but by becoming very nervous in disadvantageous situations, and conquering him by her painful condition. She never expressed her excessive jealousies, but sought to shackle him as required by her fits of anxiety. Thus, successful as he was in all but one relation of life, the man felt uncertain of having reached his goal of superiority, and his excessive ambition was demanding compensation.

I know that many psychologists would seek for a " guilt complex " to explain this depression. They would investigate the patient's childhood to find out a very early desire to kill someone—probably the father. This patient, however, had been the favourite of his father, and there was not the least reason why he should ever have desired his death, as he had always been able to manage him in his own interest. Such a mistaken search for a " guilt complex " might also lead a psychologist to think that the patient had secretly wished to murder his friend and rival : and that after having triumphed over him and having had the death-wish granted by fate, he remained still unsatisfied. If that were so, the guilt complex might be developed by the striving of the patient to see himself in an intenser light. He would want to express his good feeling and liking for his former rival with the highest sincerity and honesty ; and at the same time he would be shaken by the memory of his rival's fatal end and the thoughts which he had been unable wholly to dismiss before it happened. This would amount to the complicated state of self-accusation and repentance at the same time, which we call a guilt complex, which is always a superiority-striving on the useless side of life. As I have already observed, it means: " I have reached the summit of error " or " My virtue is so lofty that this slight stain upon it is killing me."

However, in this case I found no indications of the kind, and the man's valuation of honesty as a virtue was not abnormally developed. His depressions were an attempt to show himself superior to his wife. To be depressed in very favourable situations called attention to his good fortune much more than if he had allowed himself to enjoy them. Everyone was surprised at his depression, and he constantly asked himself, " You happy being, *why* are you depressed when you have everything you want ? " The unmanageable wife was the one sorrow in his comfortable life, and he compensated for this by *remembering his victory* in the most difficult phase of his history—when he outstripped his friend and won the woman from him. Loyalty forbade him to rejoice in the memory of his dead friend : but he could nevertheless feed upon this ancient triumph by being depressed in the box of the theatre. The more melancholy he was and upon the brighter the occasion, the more he was able to think of his past conquest and to elevate the consciousness of his estate. Deeper enquiries confirmed my conclusion. His friend had died from paralysis after syphilis, a disease which they had both contracted at the same time. My patient was cured, however ; and now, surrounded by his healthy wife and six children, could not but recall, together with the triumph over his friend, his conquest of the disease.

Such, then, were his consolations. In his marriage this man did not feel superior ; but at least his wife was the woman his friend had desired, and she had chosen him instead. By contemplating his friend's disaster in a discreet gloom he heightened the sense of victory. Consolation of this nature is on the useless side, however, and tends, as we see, towards disease.

IMPOTENCE FOLLOWED BY POLYGAMOUS DESIRES

A man of thirty-six came to me for advice about sexual impotence after having tried various treatments. He was a self-made man, in a good position, and physically healthy, but not very well educated : and he had a love relation with a well-educated girl. He was a second child between two girls, and had lost both parents at the age of five. He remembered that his family had been very poor, but that he had been a spoilt child, very pretty and quiet, to whom the neighbours liked to give presents : and that he exploited their generosity, behaving like a beggar. One of his earliest remembrances was of walking the streets on Christmas Eve and looking into the shop windows at the Christmas trees destined *for others*. In the orphanage, to which he was transferred at the age of five, he was strictly treated, but his habitual docility and the striving nature he possessed as a second child enabled him to surpass others. His servility stood him in good stead, for he was promoted to be the principal servant of the institution. In this occupation he had sometimes to wait for a long time at an old and deserted railway station in the country ; and at these times, when only the humming of the telegraph wires relieved the dead stillness of the night, he felt utterly isolated and alone in a friendless world. He preserved strong memories of this experience.

Often, in later life, he complained of buzzing in the ears, for which no aurist could find the cause. It proved, however, to be quite coherent with his style of life. When he felt isolated, which happened very often, the memory of the humming wires returned with all the liveliness of a hallucination. After this had been explained to him, and he had been a little more socially reconciled and encouraged to marry his sweetheart, the humming ceased.

It is quite usual for children who are brought up in an orphanage to make the strongest efforts to hide the fact, as though it were a disgrace. This man justified his concealment by asserting that many orphans do not succeed in later life. He regarded failure in life as the inexorable fate of orphans, which gave him his tense and striving attitude in business. For the same reason he halted before the problem of love and marriage, and his neurotic impotence was the immediate result of this profound hesitation.

This man's style of life, as we have seen, was to be a beggar. In business, however (as previously in the orphanage), begging had paved the way to domination. In business he enjoyed nothing more than a begging attitude on the part of his subordinates. He was only a beggar until he could be a conqueror, and he played the second rôle as heartily as the first. There is no need to drag in the idea of " ambivalent " characteristics, as some psychologists would do immediately. Rightly understood, the whole of this mental process—working from below to above, expressing an inferiority but compensating with a superiority—is not ambivalence but a dynamic unity. Only if it is not understood as a whole do we see it as two contradictory and warring entities. In his business we find the man with a " superiority complex " : but if he were to lose his position and have to start again he would promptly go back to the expression of inferiority and make capital out of it. In his love-problem he was, for the time being, upon the submissive line of action, begging for love, but trying to reach domination. His sweetheart liked him and wanted to marry him, so she responded to his hesitancy by taking up more and more of a begging attitude towards him ! He was well on the way, in fact, towards getting the upper hand with her, and frequently did so in minor matters.

He had still not overcome his hesitant attitude : but after having had his style of life explained to him and having been encouraged, his state improved and his impotence disappeared. He then set up a second resistance, which was that every woman attracted him, and these polygamous desires were an escape from marriage. At this time he dreamt that he was lying upon a couch in my room, and he became sexually excited and had a pollution.

There is no couch in my consulting room. My patients sit, stand, or move about as they please ; but the couch in this dream was in the room of a doctor who had formerly treated him for a few months. This dream extracted a confession which he had never made before. He believed that both the other doctor and I belonged to a secret society, the object of which was to cure patients such as himself by providing sexual intercourse for them. For this reason he had been trying to find out which of my woman patients would be chosen for him. The fact that he missed the couch in my room was like an accusation against me. I was not the right doctor. He had come to me *begging*, expecting me to settle his difficulties, take over his responsibilities, and to assist him to escape from marriage. My collusion in stopping his marriage was to go to the length of being his procurer, a fantasy to which his fright, his impotence and his polygamous tendencies were all contributory. Failing that, he would solve his sexual problem by pollutions, as others might resort to masturbation or perversion.

He married, but it was difficult to prevent him from

developing a tyrannical attitude towards his conciliatory wife.

Another case of the begging attitude was brought to me by a man fifty years old, the youngest of a very poor family. He had been indulged by his mother and the neighbours because of an apparent weakness, and early developed a very timid manner. He always tried to lean upon his mother and to appeal to the sympathies of weak persons, especially in difficult times when he exhibited great depression and cried until help came. We have already seen the use which is made of crying by both children and adults. This man's earliest memory was that he had fallen down and hurt himself. The choice of this incident to treasure in the memory out of all possible recollections is explained only by his desire to impress himself with the danger of life. His technique of life was to perfect himself in the rôle of a beggar, to attract support, consolation and favour by calling attention to his infirmities. Every incident was made into a matter for tears.

As a child the man had been very backward in learning to talk, and his mother, as always happens in such cases, had to attend all the more carefully to him to find out what he wanted. In this way he was able to feel like a little king. As Lessing said, " The real beggar is the only real king." He became a master of the begging art, expressing his inferiority in the power of his plight over others. " How can I make the poor weak child a king ? " was the problem of life as he saw it, and he answered it by elaborating his own individual and essentially mendicant style.

This is one way of living, and so early an apprentice becomes a past master of its technique. He will not change it, unless the cost becomes clearly too great, when he may be brought to see that his childish method is inadequate for present problems. Otherwise change is impossible for him, because he has all his life ascribed every success to the begging art and every failure to lack of proficiency in it. Such a goal as this is not calculable from the inheritance or the environmental stimuli, for the child's individual conception of the future is the dominant causal factor, and this patient's conception was such that whenever he wanted to attain superiority he had to make a mistake or get himself into a mess of some kind. All his feelings were appropriately ordered towards the goal of thus getting something for nothing.

After a few days' treatment this man was very much impressed by what I told him ; and he sent me a pamphlet he had written some years before. It was entitled " An Association of Beggars."

––––––

Habitual criticism, anger, and envy are indications of a useless striving for superiority : they are motions towards the suppression of others, either in reality or fancy, so as to be supreme. Useful criticism of a constructive tendency is always in some comprehensible relation with social feeling, but where the motive is merely relative self-elevation by lowering or degrading others the tendency is neurotic. Neurotics often make use of the truth in order to undervalue others, and it is important, when checking a neurotic criticism, not to overlook the element of truth in the observation.

Anger is usually a sign that the person who is angry feels at a disadvantage—at least temporarily. Neurotics use it freely as a weapon to intimidate those who are responsible for them. Although occasional anger is an understandable attitude in certain critical relations, when it is habitual it is a sign of anxiety, of impatience, or of feelings of helplessness or suppression. Patients of this habit are often very clever in the selection of vulnerable points to attack in others, and are also great strategists in preparing such situations that they put others slightly in the wrong before they begin a fight.

Envy is universally an expression of inferiority, though it may sometimes be a stimulus to useful action. In neurosis, however, envy of another's good does not go so far as practical emulation. It stops like a tram before the journey's end, leaving the patient irritable and depressed.

In a certain popular music-hall turn the " strong man " comes on and lifts an enormous weight with care and immense difficulty, and then, during the hearty applause of the audience, a child comes in and gives away the fraud by carrying the dummy weight off with one hand. There are plenty of neurotics who swindle us with such weights, and who are adepts in the art of appearing over-burdened. They could really dance with the load under which they stagger like Atlas bearing the world on his shoulders. Yet it cannot be denied that neurotics feel their burden very keenly. They may be continually tired. They may sometimes perspire very freely, and their symptoms may suggest the possibility of tuberculosis. Every movement is very tiring, and they often suffer from palpitation of the heart. Usually depressed, they continually demand more zealous care from others, and yet find it continually insufficient.

AGORAPHOBIA: AVOIDANCE OF PEOPLE

I had a case of agoraphobia in a man of fifty-three, who found that he could not breathe properly when he was in company with others. He was living with his sister, and had a son whose characteristics were very much like his own. When I investigated the cause of this man's unusual concentration of interest upon himself, I found that he had been orphaned at ten years of age, and there were two elder brothers in the home. It was when they quarrelled that he had had his first attack. This indicates the tendency to meet a difficult situation by breakdown. The man was the youngest of a family of eight, and educated by his grandfather. A grand-parent is almost invariably a spoiling foster-parent. The patient's father and mother had been happily married ; the father was superior and the mother rather cold, so the boy was attracted to his father.

A child's first good-fellowship in life is always with the mother if she is present, so that if it inclines more towards the father we may assume that the mother does not give the child sufficient attention : she is probably unkind, otherwise occupied, or more attentive to a younger child. In such circumstances the child turns to the father if possible, and in this case the resistance to the mother was very marked.

People are often unable correctly to remember their earliest situations, but experience enables us to reconstruct their circumstances from comparatively slight indications. One man said he could only remember three incidents from early childhood which had deeply impressed his memory. The first of these occurred at the age of three, when his brother died. He was with his grandfather on the day of the funeral, when his mother returned from the cemetery, sorrowful and sobbing, and when the grandfather kissed her, whispering some words of kindness and consolation, the boy saw that his mother smiled a little. He was very much upset by this, and for long afterwards resented his mother's smile on the day that her child was buried. A second memory that he had preserved was of a friendly reproof from his uncle, who had asked him, " Why are you always so rough towards your mother ? " A third remembrance from the same period of his life related to a quarrel between his parents, after which he turned to his father, saying, " You were brave, daddy, like a soldier ! " He depended much upon his father, and was pampered by him : and he always admired his father more than his mother, although he realised that his mother's character was of a better type.

All these memories, which appeared to date from his third or fourth year, showed the fighting attitude towards the mother. The first and the third remembrances were clearly ruled by his goal, which was to criticise the mother and to justify him in turning towards the father. His reason for turning away from the mother is easy to guess : he had been too much spoilt by her to be able to put up with the younger brother's appearance upon the scene,—that same younger brother who figures in an apparently innocent manner in the first recollection.

This patient had married at the age of twenty-four, and marriage had disappointed him, because of his wife's demands upon him. Marriage between two spoilt children is always unhappy, because both remain in the expectant attitude and neither begins to give. This man went through varied experiences and tried different occupations without success. His wife was not sympathetic, and complained that she would rather be the mistress of a rich man than the wife of a poor one, and the union ended in a divorce. Although the man was not really poor, he was very stingy towards his wife, and she divorced him by way of revenge.

After his divorce he turned misogynistic, and developed homosexual tendencies ; he had no actual relationships with men, but felt a desire to embrace men. This homosexual trend was as usual a kind of cowardliness. He had been twice defeated and baulked by women—first by his mother and afterwards by his wife—and he was now trying to divert his sexuality towards men so as to evade women and further possibilities of humiliation. To confirm himself in such a tendency a man can easily falsify the past by recollecting and magnifying the importance of certain common experiences which are then taken by him as proofs of inborn homosexual tendencies. Thus, this patient remembered that he had been in love with a schoolmaster, and that in his youth a boy friend had seduced him into mutual masturbation.

The determining factor in this man's behaviour was that he was a spoiled child who wanted everything for nothing. His agoraphobia resulted from the fear of meeting women on the one hand, and on the other hand it was also dangerous to meet men, because of possible erotic inclination towards them. In this tension of feelings about going out of doors he developed stomach and respiratory troubles. Many nervous people begin to swallow air when they get into a state of tension, which causes flatulence, stomach trouble, anxiety and palpitation, besides affecting the breathing. When I made him realise that this was his condition he asked the usual question : " What shall I do not to swallow air ? " Sometimes I reply : " I can tell you how to mount a horse, but I can't tell you how *not* to mount a horse." Or sometimes I advise : " If you want to go out, and feel in a conflict about it, swallow some air quickly." This man, like some other patients, swallowed air even in sleep, but after my advice he began to control himself, and discontinued the habit. Air-swallowing at night and vomiting upon waking occur in these patients who suffer from stomach trouble and anxiety when they are bothered by a difficulty which must be confronted upon the following day. The patient in question began to recuperate when he came to understand that, as a pampered child, he expected continually to take without giving. He now realised that he had first stopped his normal sexual life, looking for something easier, and afterwards adopted a fictitious homosexuality in which he also stopped short of danger, the whole process being an elaborate way of coming to a standstill. The last obstacle to be removed was his fear of mixing with strangers who did not care for him, such as the people in the streets. This fear is produced by the deeper motive of agoraphobia, which is to exclude all situations in which one is not the centre of attention.

VII

The Family Constellation

It is a common fallacy to imagine that children of the same family are formed in the same environment. Of course there is much which is the same for all in the same home, but the psychic situation of each child is individual and differs from that of others, because of the order of their succession.

There has been some misunderstanding of my custom of classification according to position in the family. It is not, of course, the child's number in the order of successive births which influences its character, but the situation into which it is born. Thus, if the eldest child is feeble-minded or suppressed, the second child may acquire a style of life similar to that of an eldest child; and in a large family, if two are born much later than the rest, and grow up together separated from the older children, the older of these may develop like a first child. This also happens sometimes in the case of twins.

The first child has the unique position of having been

alone at the beginning. Being thus a central interest he is generally spoiled. In this he resembles the only child, and spoiling is almost inevitable in both cases. The first child, however, usually suffers an important change of situation, being dethroned when the second baby is born. The child is generally quite unprepared for this change, and feels that he has lost his position as the centre of love and attention. Great tension then arises in his mind, and a striving to regain favour. He uses all the means by which he has hitherto attracted notice. Of course he would like to go the best way about it, to be beloved for his goodness : but this is apt to pass unnoticed when everyone is busied with the new-comer ; and he is then likely to change his tactics, to resort to old activities which attracted even unfavourable attention, and to increase these more and more. If intelligent, he acts intelligently, but not in harmony with the family's demands. Antagonism, disobedience, attacks on the baby, or even attempts to play the part of a baby, compel the parents to reconsider his existence. He must have the spot-light upon himself, even at the cost of expressing weakness or imitating a return to babyhood. Thus, hypnotised by the past, he attains his goal in the present by unsuitable means : suddenly showing inability to function alone, needing assistance in eating and excretion and requiring to be constantly watched, or compelling solicitude by getting into danger and terrifying the parents. The appearance of such characteristics as jealousy, envy or egoism has an obvious relation to the circumstances, but he may also indulge in—or prolong—illnesses such as asthma and whooping-cough. The tension in certain types may produce headache, migraine, stomach trouble, petit mal, and hysterical chorea. Slighter symptoms are evinced in a tired appearance and a general change of behaviour for the worse, with which the child impresses his parents. Naturally, the later the rival baby is born, the more intelligent and understandable will be the first child's change in behaviour. If dethroned very early, the eldest child's efforts are of a more instinctive character. The style of his striving will in any case be conditioned by the reaction of others in the environment and the way in which he estimates it. If, for instance, the dethroned child finds that he can win in a fight, he will become a fighting child : if fighting does not pay, he may lose hope, become depressed, and score a success by worrying and frightening the parents, after which he will resort to ever more subtle uses of misfortune to gain his end.

The activity of such a prototype in later life was shown in the case of a man who became afraid to swallow for fear of choking. Why did he select this symptom instead of another ? The patient had an immediate social difficulty in the behaviour of an intimate friend, who attacked him violently. Both the patient and his wife had come to the conclusion that he must put up with it no longer, but he did not feel strong enough to face the struggle. Upon enquiry into his childhood, it appeared that he had had such a difficulty about swallowing before. He was the eldest child, and had been surpassed by his younger brother, and then he had been able, by this difficulty in eating, to make his father and mother watch over him. Now faced with a personal defeat in later life, and not knowing what to do about it, he fell back upon this old line of defence, as though it might make someone watch over him and help him.

The dethronement of the first child by another may make it turn away from the mother towards the father, and a very critical attitude towards the mother will then persist ever after. A person of this type is always afraid of being put back in life ; and we notice that in all his affairs he likes to make one step forward and then one backward, so that nothing decisive can happen. He always feels justified in fearing that a favourable situation will change. Towards all the three life-questions he will take up a hesitative attitude, with certain problematic and neurotic tendencies. The latter will be felt by him as a help and a security. He will approach society, for example, with a hostile attitude ; in regard to his occupation, he will be always changing ; and in his erotic life he will find lack of function, and polygamous tendencies—if he falls in love with one person he very quickly falls in love with another. Dubious and unwilling to decide anything, he becomes a great procrastinator. I had a very perfect example of this type once, and his earliest remembrance was this : " At three years of age I caught scarlet fever. My mother gave me the carbolic acid in mistake for a gargle, and I nearly died." He had a younger sister who was the favourite of his mother. Later in life this patient had developed a curious fantasy of a young girl ruling and bullying an older one. Sometimes he imagined her riding the old woman like a horse.

CRUELTY IN A SECOND BORN

The eldest child may, however, be so firmly fixed in the parents' favour that he cannot be supplanted. This may be either by virtue of his own good endowment and development, or by the second child's inferiority, if the latter is ugly, organically handicapped, or badly brought up. In such a case it is the second child who becomes the problem, and the eldest may have a very satisfactory development, as in the following case :—

Of two brothers, differing four years in age, the older had

been much attached to the mother, and when the younger was born the father had been ill for some time, which took the entire time and most of the attention of the mother. The older boy, trained in friendship and obedience to her, tried to help and relieve her, and the younger boy was put into the care of a nurse, who spoiled him. This situation lasted for some years, so that the younger child had no reasonable chance to compete with the older for the love of the mother ; and he soon abandoned the useful side of life, and became wild and disobedient. His behaviour became still worse four years later, when a little sister was born, to whom the mother was able to devote herself owing to the death of the father. Thus twice excluded from the mother's attention and spoiled by the nurse, we need not be surprised that this second child was the worst pupil in his class, whilst the elder boy was always the best. Feeling hopelessly handicapped in competition with his brother, unloved at home, and reproached at the school (from which he was finally expelled), this second son could find no goal in life but to worry his mother. Being physically stronger than both the brother and the sister, he took to tyrannising over them. He trifled away his time, and at puberty he began to waste money and to incur debts. His honest and well-meaning parents provided a very strict tutor for him who did not, of course, grasp the situation, and dealt with it superficially by punishments. So the boy grew into a man who strove to get rich quickly and easily. He fell an easy prey to unscrupulous advisers, followed them into fruitless enterprises, and not only lost his money but involved his parents in his dishonourable debts.

The facts of the case clearly showed that all the courage this man ever had was dictated by his unsatisfied desire to conquer. This was most clearly shown in a queer game which he played from time to time, especially when things went against him. His nurse was now an old woman, earning her living in the family as a superior servant, and she still worshipped the second boy and always interceded for him in his numerous scrapes. The odd sport in which he indulged was to lock her in a room with him and make her play at soldiers with him, commanding her to march, to fall and to jump up again at his orders ; and sometimes he quickened her obedience by beating her with a stick. She always obeyed although she screamed and resisted.

This singular sport revealed what he really wanted, the completest domination in the easiest way. Some writers would describe this as sadistic conduct, but I demur at the use of a word which implies a sexual interest, for I could discover nothing of the kind in it. In sexual matters the man was practically normal, except that he changed his objective too frequently and always chose inferiors. Genuine sadism itself is a domineering tendency availing itself of the sexual urge for its expression, owing to the discouragement of the individual in other spheres.

In the end this man brought himself into very bad circumstances, while the elder brother became very successful and highly respected.

––––––

The eldest child, partly because he often finds himself acting as representative of the parental authority, is normally a great believer in power and the laws. The intuitive perception of this fact is shown in the ancient and persistent custom of primogeniture. It is often observable in literature. Thus Theodore Fontane wrote of his perplexity at his father's pleasure in hearing that ten thousand Poles had defeated twenty thousand Russians. His father was a French emigrant who had sided with the Poles, but to the writer it was an inconceivable idea that the stronger could be beaten ; he felt that might must, and ought to, succeed.   This was because Theodore Fontane was a first child.   In any case the eldest child is readier than others to recognise power, and likes to support it.   This is shown in the lives of scientists, politicians, and artists, as well as in those of simpler people. Even if the person is a revolutionary we find a conservative tendency, as in the case of Robespierre.

The second child is in a very different situation, never having had the experience of being the only one.   Though he is also petted at first, he is never the sole centre of attention.   Life from the first is more or less of a race ; the first child sets the pace, and the second tries to surpass him. What results from the competition between two such children depends on their courage and self-confidence.   If the elder becomes discouraged he will be in a serious situa- tion, especially if the younger is really strong and outstrips him.

If the second child loses hope of equality he will try to *shine* more rather than to *be* more.   That is, if the elder is too strong for him, the younger will tend to escape to the useless side of life, and in our problem cases laziness, lying or stealing will begin to pave the way towards neurosis, crime and self-destruction.

As a rule, however, the second child is in a better position than the first.   His pace-maker stimulates him to effort. Also, it is a common thing for the first child to hasten his own dethronement by fighting against it with envy, jealousy and truculence, which lower him in the parental favour.   It is when the first child is brilliant that the second child is in the worst situation.

TO BE CLEANER THAN EVERYBODY ELSE

But the elder child is not always the worst sufferer, even when dethroned. I saw this in the case of a girl who had been the centre of attention and extremely spoiled until she reached the age of three, when a sister was born. After the birth of her sister she became very jealous and developed into a problem-child. The younger sister grew up with sweet and charming manners, and was much the more beloved of the two. But when this younger sister came to school the situation was not to her taste : she was no longer spoiled, and being unprepared to encounter difficulties was frightened and tried to withdraw. To escape defeat both in fact and in appearance, she adopted a device very common among the discouraged—she never finished anything she was doing, so that it always escaped final judgment, and she wasted as much time as possible. We find that time is the great enemy of such people, for under social conditions they feel as if time were persecuting them continually with the question, " How will you use me ? " Hence their strange efforts to " kill time " with silly activities. This girl always came late and postponed every action. She did not antagonise anyone, even if reproved, but her charm and sweetness, which were maintained as before, did not prevent her from being a greater worry and burden than her fighting sister.

When the elder sister became engaged to be married the younger was desperately unhappy. Though she had won the first stage of the race with her rival by gentleness and obedience, she had given up in the later stages of school and social life. She felt her sister's marriage as a defeat, and that her only hope of regaining ground would be to marry also. However, she had not courage enough to choose a suitable partner, and instinctively sought a second-best. First she fell in love with a man suffering seriously from tuberculosis. Can we regard this as a step forward ? Does it contradict her pre-established custom of leaving every task unfinished ? Not at all : the poor health of her lover and her parents' natural resistance to the match were sure causes of delay and frustration. She preferred an element of impossibility in her choice. Another scarcely eligible partner appeared later in her life, in a man thirty years older than herself and apparently senile. However, this one did not die, and the marriage took place : but it was not a great success for her, as the attitude of hopelessness in which she had trained herself did not allow her any useful activity. It also inhibited her sexual life which she considered disgusting, and felt humiliated and soiled by it. She used her usual methods to evade love and postpone relations at the appropriate times. She did not quite succeed in this, however, and became pregnant, which she regarded as another hopeless event, and from that time onward not only rejected caresses but complained that she felt soiled, and began to wash and clean all day long. She not only washed herself, but cleaned everything that had been touched by her husband, by the maidservant or the visitors, including furniture, linen, and shoes. Soon she allowed no one to touch any of the objects in her room, and lived in a neurosis of washing-compulsion. Thus she was excused from the solution of her problems, and attained a very lofty goal of superiority—she felt more fastidiously clean than anyone else.

Exaggerated striving for a lofty goal of high distinctiveness is well expressed in the neurosis of " washing-compulsion." As far as I have been able to ascertain, this illness is always used as a means of avoiding sexual relations, and invariably gives the fantastic compensation of feeling cleaner than everybody else.

———————

By this feeling for life as a race, however, the second child usually trains himself more stiffly, and if his courage holds is well on the way to overcome the eldest on his own ground. If he has a little less courage he will choose to surpass the eldest in another field, and if still less, he will become more critical and antagonistic than usual, not in an objective but in a personal manner. In childhood this attitude appears towards trifles : he will want the window shut when the elder opens it, turn on the light when the other wants it extinguished, and be consistently contrary and opposite.

This situation is well described in the Biblical story of Esau and Jacob, where Jacob succeeds in usurping the privileges of the eldest. The second child's condition is like that of an engine under a constantly excessive head of steam. It was well expressed by a little boy of four, who cried out, weeping, " I am so unhappy because I can *never* be as old as my brother."

The fact that children repeat the psychic behaviour of older brothers and sisters and of parents is referred by some writers to an instinct of imitation or to " identification " of the self with another : but it is better explained as a way of asserting an equality which is denied on other grounds. Psychic resemblances to the conduct of ancestors or even of savages do not signify that the pattern of psychic reaction is hereditary, but that many individuals use the same means of offence and defence in similar situations. When we find so much resemblance between all first children, all second and all youngest children, we may well ask what part is left for heredity to play. Thus we have also no use, as psychologists, for the theory that the mental development of the individual ought to repeat the development of the race of mankind in successive stages.

In later development, the second child is rarely able to endure the strict leadership of others or to accept the idea of " eternal laws." He will be much more inclined to believe, rightly or wrongly, that there is no power in the world which cannot be overthrown. Beware of his revolutionary subtleties ! I have known quite a few cases in which the second child has availed himself of the strangest means to undermine the power of ruling persons or traditions. Not everybody, certainly not these rebels themselves, would easily agree with my view of their behaviour. For though it is possible to endanger a ruling power with slander, there are more insidious ways—for example, by means of excessive praise—you may idealise and glorify a man or a method until the reality cannot stand up to it. Both methods are employed in Mark Antony's oration in " Julius Cæsar," and I have shown elsewhere how Fedor Dostoevsky made masterly use of the latter means, perhaps unconsciously, to undermine the pillars of old Russia.[1] Those who remember his representation of Father Zosima in " The Brothers Karamazov," and also recall the fact that he was a second son, will allow the force of my suggestion.

I need hardly say that the style of life of a second child, like that of the first, may also appear in another child if the situation is of a similar pattern.

The youngest child is also a distinct type, exhibiting certain characteristics of style which we never fail to find.

[1] "Dostoevsky." In Alfred Adler, *The Practice and Theory of Individual Psychology* (1925). Paterson, N. J.: Littlefield, Adams, 1959. pp. 280–290.

He has always been the baby of the family, and has never known the tragedy of being dispossessed by a younger, which is more or less the fate of all other children. In this respect his situation is a favoured one, and his education is often relatively better, as the economic position of the family is likely to be more secure in its later years. The grown-up children not infrequently join with the parents in spoiling the youngest child, who is thus liable to be too much indulged. On the other hand the youngest may also be too much stimulated by elders—both mistakes are well known to our educationists. In the former case (of over-indulgence) the child will strive throughout life to be supported by others. In the latter case the child will rather resemble a second child, proceeding competitively, striving to overtake all those who set the pace for him, and in most cases failing to do so. Often, therefore, he looks for a field of activity remote from that of the other members of the family—in which, I believe, he gives a sign of hidden cowardice. If the family is commercial, for instance, the youngest inclines to art or poetry ; if scientific, he wants to be a salesman. I have remarked elsewhere that many of the most successful men of our time were youngest children, and I am convinced this is also the case in any other age. In Biblical history we find a remarkable number of youngest children among the leading characters, such as David, Saul, and Joseph. The story of Joseph is a particularly good example, and illustrates many of the views we have advanced. His younger brother Benjamin was seventeen years his junior, and when he reached the height of his powers Joseph did not know of the existence of this younger brother. His psychological position, therefore, was that of a youngest child.

It is interesting to note how well Joseph's brethren understood his dreams. More precisely, I should say that they understood the feeling and emotion of the dreamer, a point to which I shall return later. The purpose of a dream is not to be understood but to create a mood and a tension of feeling.

In the fairy tales of all ages and peoples the youngest child plays the rôle of a conqueror. I infer that in earlier times, when both circumstances and men's apprehension of them were simpler, it was easier to collect experiences and to understand the coherent current of the life of the latest-born. This traditional grasp of character survives in folk-lore when the actual experiences are forgotten.

THE PHYSICIAN LOOKED AFTER BY HIS OLDER SISTERS

A strange case of the type of youngest child who is spoiled is that which I have already given, of a man with a " begging " style of life. I came across another in the difficulties of a physician who had for twenty years been unable to swallow normally and could take only liquid food. He had recently had a dental plate made for him, which he was continually pushing up and down with his tongue, a habit which caused pain and soreness of the tongue, so that he feared he was developing cancer.

He was the youngest of a family of three, with two older sisters, and had been weakly and much indulged. At the age of forty he could only eat alone or with his sisters. This is a clear indication that he was only comfortable in his favourite situation—of being spoiled by the sisters. Every approach to society had been difficult, and he had no friends, and only a few associates whom he met weekly in a restaurant. His attitude towards the three questions of life being one of fear and trembling, we can understand that his tension with other people made him unable to swallow food. He lived in a kind of stage fright, fearful that he was not making a sufficiently good impression.

This man answered the second life-question (of occupation) with tolerable competence, because his origin was a poor one and he could not live without earning, but he suffered exceedingly in his profession, and nearly fainted when he had to take his examinations. His ambition, as a general practitioner, was to obtain a position with a fixed salary, and, later on, a pension. This attraction to an official position is a sign of insecurity, and people with a deep sense of inadequacy commonly aspire to the " safe job." For years he gave himself up to his symptoms. When he became older he lost some of his teeth, and decided to have a plate made, which became the occasion of his latest symptom.

When he came to me, the patient was sixty years of age, and still living in the care of his two sisters. Both were suffering from their age, and it was clear to me that this man, ageing, and spoiled by two unmarried and much older women, was facing a new situation. He was very much afraid his sisters would die. What should he do in that case—he who needed to be continually noticed and watched over ? He had never been in love, for he could never find a woman whom he could trust with his fragile happiness ! How could he believe that anyone would spoil him as his mother and elder sisters had done ? It was easy to guess the form of his sexuality—masturbation, and some petting affairs with girls ; but recently an older woman had wanted to marry him ; and he wished to appear more pleasant and attractive in behaviour. The beginning of a struggle seemed imminent, but his new dental plate came to the rescue. In the nick of time he became anxious about contracting cancer of the tongue.

He himself, as a doctor, was very much in doubt about the reality of this cancer. The many surgeons and physicians he consulted all tried to dissuade him from belief in it, but he persisted in his uncertainty, continued to press his tongue against the plate until he hurt it, and then consulted another doctor.

Such pre-occupations—" over-valued ideas," as Wernicke calls them—are carefully cherished in the arrangement of a neurosis. The patient shies away from the right objective by fixing his glances more and more firmly upon a point somewhere off his course. He does this in order to swerve out of a direction which is beginning to be indicated by logical necessity. The logical solution of his problem would be antagonistic to his style of life, and as the style of life must rule he has to establish emotions and feelings which will ensure his escape.

In spite of the fact that this man was sixty years old, the only logical solution of his problem was to find a trustworthy substitute for his spoiling sisters before their departure. His distrustful mind could not rise to the hope of its possibility ; nor could his doubts be dissipated by logic, because he had built up his whole life with a definite resistance to marriage. The dental plate, which should have been a help towards marriage, became an insuperable impediment to it.

In the treatment of this case it was useless to attack the belief in the cancer. When he understood the coherence of his behaviour the patient's symptoms were very much alleviated. The next day he told me of a dream : " I was sitting in the house of a third sister at a birthday celebration of her thirteen-year-old son. I was entirely healthy, felt no pain, and could swallow anything." But this dream was related to an episode in his life which took place fifteen years before. Its meaning is very obvious : "*If only I were fifteen years younger.*" Thus is the style maintained.

The only child also has his typical difficulties. Retaining the centre of the stage without effort, and generally pampered, he forms such a style of life that he will be supported by others and at the same time rule them. Very often he grows up in an intimate environment. The parents may be afraid to have more children, and sometimes the mother, neurotic before his advent, does not feel equal to rearing more children, and develops such behaviour that everyone must say, " It is a blessing that this woman has no more children." Birth-control may absorb much of the attention of the family, in which case we may infer tension, and the two parents united to carry on their life in anxiety. The care then devoted to the only child never ceases by day or night, and often impresses the child with a belief that it is an almost mortal danger not to be watched and guarded. Such children often grow up cautious, and sooner or later they are often successful and gain the esteem and attention they desire. But if they come into wholly different conditions of life they may show striking insufficiency.

Only children are often very sweet and affectionate, and later in life they may develop charming manners in order to appeal to others, as they train themselves in this way, both in early life and later. They are usually closer to the more indulgent parent, which is generally the mother ; and in some cases develop a hostile attitude towards the other parent.

The education of the only child is not easy, but it is possible to understand the individual problem and to solve it correctly. We do not regard the only child's situation as dangerous, but we find that, in the absence of the best educational methods, very bad results occur which would have been avoided if there had been brothers and sisters.

THE DRESSMAKER'S ONLY CHILD, A SON

I will give a case of the development of an only child, a boy whose attachment was entirely to the mother. The father was of no importance in the family ; he maintained them, but was obviously without interest in the child. The mother was a dressmaker who worked at home, and the little boy spent all his time with her, sitting or playing beside her. He played at sewing, imitating his mother's activity, and ultimately became very proficient in it, but he never took any part in boys' games. The mother left the house each day at five p.m. to deliver her work, and returned punctually at six, and during that time the boy was left alone or with an older niece, and played with sewing materials. He became interested in timepieces, because he was always looking for his mother's return. He could tell the time at three years old.

The older niece played games with him in which she was the bridegroom and he was the bride, and it is noteworthy that he looked more like a girl than she did. When he came to school he was quite unprepared to associate with boys, but he was able to establish himself as a favoured exception, for others liked his mild and courteous disposition. He began to approach the goal of superiority by being attractive, especially so towards boys and men. At fourteen years of age he acted the part of a girl in a school play. The audience had not the slightest doubt that he was a girl, a young fellow began to flirt with him, and he was much pleased to have excited such admiration.

He declared that he had only known the difference of sex for a short time. He had worn girlish dress for four years, and until the age of ten he did not know whether he was a boy or a girl. When his sex was explained to him he began to masturbate, and in his fantasy he soon connected sexual desire with what he had felt when boys touched him or kissed him. To be admired and wooed was the goal in life to which he accommodated all his characteristics, so that he might be admired by boys. His older niece was the only girl he had known, and she was gentle and sweet, but she played the man's rôle in their games and otherwise she ruled him like his mother. A great feeling of inferiority was his legacy from his mother's over-indulgent and excessive care. She had married late, at the age of thirty-eight, and she did not wish to have more children by the husband she disliked. Her anxiety, then, was doubtless of earlier origin, and her late marriage indicative of a hesitant attitude to life. Very strict in sexual matters, she wanted her child to be educated in ignorance of sex.

At the age of sixteen this patient looked and walked like a flirtatious girl, and he soon fell into the snare of homosexuality. In order to comprehend this development we must remember that he had had, in a psychological sense, the education of a girl, and that the difference between the sexes was realised too late in his development. Also he had his triumphs in the feminine rôle, and no certainty of gaining as much by playing the man. In the imitation of girlish behaviour he could not but see an open road to his goal of superiority.

It is my experience that boys who have this type of education always look like girls. The growth of the organs and probably also of the glands is partially ruled by the environment and adapted to it ; so that if such an early bent towards feminity is succeeded by a personal goal of the same tendency, the wish to be a favoured girl will influence not only the mind, but also the carriage and even the body.

This case illustrates very clearly how a pervert trains himself mentally into his abnormal attitude towards sex. There is no necessity to postulate an inborn or hereditary constitution. This patient's exclusion of all normal sexual activity, both mental and physical, in favour of masturbation and homosexuality, might cause suspicion of an inherited component except that we can catch him in the very act of perverting himself. In the homosexual circles of different localities there are different traditions, and this boy had to adapt his taste to the customary practice of his homosexual associates. Nearly all those in his city practised fellatio. At first he resisted this, but one night he woke up with a queer taste in his mouth. On the table by his bed he found a glass partly filled with urine, and was not sure how it came to be there. Probably during sleep, but there was no doubt about what had happened. From this time onward he conformed with his friends : he had overcome his resistance.

When he came to me he was involved with another boy who was the neglected second child of a very domineering mother : this boy's striving was to overcome men by his personal charm, in which he actually succeeded in his relationship with a weak father. When he reached the age of sexual expression he was shocked. His notion of women was founded upon experience of his domineering mother, who neglected him ; so he turned homosexual. Consider then the hopeless situation of my patient ! He wanted to conquer by female means—by having the charm of a girl—but his friend wanted to be a conqueror of men.

I was able to make my patient realise that, whatever he himself thought or felt in this *liaison*, his friend felt himself to be a conquering man-charmer. My patient, therefore, could not be sure that his was the real conquest, and his homosexuality was accordingly checked. By this means I was able to break off the relationship, for he saw that it was stupid to enter into such a fruitless competition. This also made it easier for him to understand that his abnormality was due to a lack of interest in others, and that his feeling of inadequacy, as a pampered child, had led him to measure everything in terms of personal triumph. He then left me for some months, and when he visited me again he had had sexual relations with a girl, but had tried to play a masochistic part towards her. He obviously wished to experience with her the same inferiority that he had felt with his mother and the niece. This masochistic attitude was shown in the fact that his goal of superiority required that the girl should do to him what he commanded, and he wished to complete the act at this point, without achieving sexual intercourse, so that the normal was still excluded.

The great difficulty of changing a homosexual lies not only in his lack of social adjustment, but in the invariable absence of the right training, which ought to begin in early childhood. The attitude towards the other sex is strained in a mistaken direction almost from the beginning of life. In order to realise this fact one must note the kind of intelligence, of behaviour, and of expectations which a case exhibits. Compare normal persons walking in the street or

mixing in society with a homosexual in the same situations !
The normal are chiefly interested in the opposite sex, the
homosexual only in their own.   The latter evade normal
sexuality not only in behaviour but even in dreams.   The
patient I have just described used frequently to dream that
he was climbing a mountain, and ascending it by a serpen-
tine road.   The dream expresses his discouraged and
circuitous approach to life.   He moved rather like a snake,
bending his head and shoulders at every step.

————

In conclusion I will recall the most disastrous cases I have
known in the development of only children.   A woman
asked me to help her and her husband in the case of their
only boy, who tyrannised over them terribly.   He was then
sixteen, a very good pupil at school, but quarrelsome and
insulting in behaviour.   He specially affronted his father,
who had been stricter with him than the mother.   He
antagonised both parents continually, and if he could not
get what he wanted he was openly injurious, sometimes
wrestling with his father, spitting at him, and using bad
language.   Such a development is possible to a pampered
and only child who is trained to expect everything—and
gets it, until the time comes when indulgence can go on no
longer.   In such cases it is difficult to treat the patient in
his old environment, because too many old recollections are
revived, which disturb the harmony of the family.

Another case was brought to me, of a boy of eighteen,
who had been accused of murdering his father.   He was
an only child, and spoiled, who had stopped his education
and wasted all the money he could extort from his parents
in bad company.   One day when his father refused to give
him money, the boy killed him by hitting him on the head

with a hammer. No one but the lawyer who was defending him knew that he had killed another person several months before. It was obvious that he felt perfectly sure of escaping discovery this second time.

In yet another case of criminal development, an only boy was brought up by a very well-educated woman who wanted him to be a genius. At her death another experienced woman continued his nurture in the same way, until she became aware of his tyrannical tendencies. She believed it to be due to sexual repression, and analysed him. His tyrannical attitude did not cease, however, and she then wished to be rid of him. But he broke into her house one night intending to rob her, and throttled her.

All the characteristics which I have described as typical of certain positions in the family are liable to modification by other circumstances. With all their possibilities of variation, however, the outlines of these patterns of behaviour will be found to be substantially correct. Amongst other possibilities, one may mention the position of a boy growing up among girls. If he is older than they are he develops very much the same as an older brother close to a younger sister. Differences in age, in the affection of the parents, and in the preparation for life, are all reflected in the individual pattern of behaviour.

Where a female majority dominates the whole environment, a single boy is likely to have a goal of superiority and a style of life which are directed towards the female. This occurs in various degrees : in a humble devotion to women and worship of them, in an imitative attitude, tending towards homosexuality, or in a tyrannical attitude towards women. People usually avoid educating boys in a too female environment, and it is a matter of general experience that such children develop towards two extremes—either exaggerated vanity or audacity. In the story of Achilles there are many points from which we may assume that the latter case was well understood in antiquity.

We find the same contradictory possibilities in the cases of girls who grow up among boys or in a wholly masculine environment. In such circumstances a girl may be spoiled with too much affection, of course, but she may also adopt boys' attitudes and wish to avoid looking like a girl. In any case, what happens is largely dependent upon how men and women are valued in the environment. There is always a prevailing attitude of mind in regard to this question, largely in accordance with which the child will wish to assume the rôle of a man or of a woman.

Other views of life which prevail in the family may also influence the pattern of a child's behaviour, or bring it into difficulties, as for example the superstition about inherited characteristics, and the belief in fancy methods of education. Any exaggerated method of education is liable to cause injury to the child, a fact we can often trace in the children of teachers, psychologists, doctors, and people engaged in the administration of laws—policemen, lawyers, officers, and clergymen. Such educational exaggerations often come to light in the anamnesis of problem-children, delinquents, and neurotics. The influence of both factors—the heredity superstition and a fanatical mode of training—appear in the following case.

MOTHER ADMITTING HER MISTAKE TO DAUGHTER

A woman came to me with a daughter of nine, both of them in tears and desperation. The mother told me that the girl had only recently come to live with her, after having spent years under the care of foster-parents in the country.

There she had completed the third grade of her schooling, and she entered the fourth grade in the city school, but her work became so bad that her teacher had her put back into the third grade. Soon afterwards her work had become still worse, and she was graded still lower and put in the second. The mother was thoroughly upset at this, and obsessed with the idea that her daughter's deficiency was inherited from the father.

At first sight it was evident to me that the mother was treating the child with exaggerated educational insistence, which in this case was particularly unfortunate, because the girl had been brought up in a congenial environment and expected still greater kindness from the mother. But in her anxiety that her child should not be a failure the mother was over-strict, and this gave the child the keenest disappointment. She developed a great emotional tension which effectually blocked her progress both at school and at home. Exhortation, reproaches, criticism, and spanking only intensified the emotion, with consequent hopelessness on both sides. To confirm my impression, I spoke with the girl alone about her foster-parents. She told me how happy her life with them had been : and then, bursting into tears, told me also how she had at first enjoyed being with her mother.

I had to make the mother understand the mistakes in which she had become involved. The girl could not be expected to put up with such a hard training ; and putting myself in her place I could perfectly understand her conduct as an intelligent reaction—that is, as a form of accusation and revenge. In a situation of this type, but where there is less social feeling, it is perfectly possible for a child to turn delinquent, neurotic, or even to attempt suicide. But in this case I was sure it would not be difficult for the girl to improve if the mother could be convinced of the truth, and impress the child with a sufficiently definite change of attitude. I therefore took the mother in hand, and explained to her that the belief in inheritance was nothing but a nuisance, after which I made her realise what her daughter had not unreasonably expected when she came to live with her, and how she must have been disappointed and shaken by such disciplinary treatment, to the point of utter inability to do what was expected of her. I wanted the mother to confess to the child that she had been mistaken and would like to reform her method, so I told her I did not really believe she could bring herself to do it, but it was what I would do in the circumstances. She answered decidedly, " I will do it." In my presence and with my help, she explained her mistake to the child, and they kissed and embraced and cried together. Two weeks later they both visited me, gay and smiling and very well satisfied. The mother brought me a message from the third-grade teacher : " A miracle must have happened. The girl is the best pupil in the class."

VIII

Early Recollections

THE significance of early recollections is one of the most important discoveries of Individual Psychology, for it has demonstrated the unconscious purpose in the choice of what is longest remembered, though the memory itself is quite conscious or easily remembered upon enquiry. Rightly understood, these conscious memories give us glimpses of depths just as profound as those which are more or less suddenly released from the unconscious during treatment.

We do not, of course, believe that all early recollections are correct records of the facts. Many are even fancied, and most perhaps are changed or distorted at a later time ; but this does not always diminish their significance. What is altered or imagined is also expressive of the patient's goal, and although there is a difference between the work of fantasy and that of memory, we can safely make use of both by relating them to our knowledge of other factors. Their worth and meaning, however, cannot be rightly estimated until we relate them to the total style of life, and recognise their unity with the individual's main line of striving towards a goal of superiority. In recollections dating from the first four or five years we find chiefly fragments of the proto-type of the individual, or useful hints as to why the life-plan was elaborated in its own particular form. Here also we may gather the surest indications of self-training to overcome deficiencies or organic difficulties in the early environment. Signs of the degree of courage and social feeling are also evident in many cases. Owing to the great number of spoiled children who come under treatment the image of the mother is rarely absent from the earliest remembrance; indeed, if I suspect the life-style of a pampered child, I can invariably guess that the patient will recall something about his mother. He will never have understood the meaning of this remembrance. For instance, he may answer to my question : " I was sitting in a room playing with a toy, and my mother was sitting close to me." He regards this recollection as if it were a thing in itself, and never thinks of its coherence in the whole structure of his psychic life ; and unfortunately many psychologists do the same. To estimate its meaning we have to relate this early pattern of perception to all we can discover of his present attitude, until we find how the one clearly mirrors the other. In this example we should begin to see this if the patient suffered from anxiety when alone. The interest in being connected with the mother may even appear in the form of fictitious remembrances, as in the patient who said to me, " You will not believe me, but I can remember being born, when my mother held me in her arms."

Very often the earliest memory of a spoilt child refers to its dispossession by the birth of a younger brother or sister, and these vary from slight and innocent statements, such as, " I recollected when my younger sister was born," to anecdotes highly significant of the attitude of the patient. A woman told me : " I remember having to watch my younger sister, who was lying on a table. She was restless and threw off the coverlets. I wanted to adjust them and pulled them away from her, upon which she fell and was hurt." This woman was forty-five when she came to me ; at school, in marriage, and throughout life she felt herself disregarded, just as in her first childhood, when she had been dethroned. A similar case, more expressive of suspicion and mistrust, was expressed by a man who said : " I was going with my mother and little brother to market. Suddenly it began to rain, and my mother took me in her arms, and then, remembering that I was the older, she put me down and took up my younger brother." Successful as he was in his life, this man distrusted everybody, especially women.

A student thirty years of age came to me in trouble because he could not face his examinations : he was in such a state of strain that he could neither sleep nor concentrate. The symptoms indicate his lack of preparation and of courage, and his age shows the distance at which he stood from the solution of the problem of occupation. He had no friends and had never fallen in love, because of his lack of social adjustment, and his sexuality was expressed in masturbation and pollutions. His earliest memory was of lying in a cot, looking round at the wallpaper and curtains. This recollection reflects the isolation of his later life, and also his interest in visual activity. He was astigmatic, and striving to compensate for this organic deficiency. We must remember, however, that every function which is strongly developed apart from any social interest may disturb the harmony of life To watch is really a worth-while activity, but it is possible for watching to become a compulsion-neurosis, when the patient barricades himself against all other activities and wants to be gratifying his eyes all day. There is a type which is only interested in seeing, but there are only a few activities in which this interest can be usefully employed, and even these cannot be found by a person who is socially maladjusted. This patient, as we have seen, had not been a real fellow-man to anyone, so that he had found no use for his peculiar interest.

The earliest remembrances not infrequently disclose an interest in movements ; such as in travelling, running, motoring or jumping. So far as we can see this is characteristic of individuals who encounter difficulties when they begin to work. I found this in the case of a man of twenty-five, the eldest son of a very religious family, who was brought to me because of misbehaviour. He was disobedient, idle, and a liar, and he had contracted debts and stolen. His sister, three years younger than himself, was a familiar type, striving, capable and well-educated, an easy winner in the race with him. His misconduct began with his adolescence, and I am aware that many psychologists would ascribe it to some sort of emotional " flare-up " caused by the growth of the sexual glands ; a theory which is all the more plausible because of the existence of premature and mischievous sexual relations in this, as in other cases. But we ask, why should the perfectly natural crisis of puberty be the cause of moral disaster in this case and not in another—not in the sister's case, for example ? We answer, because the sister was in a more favourable position, and the brother's situation was one which we know, from experience of very many cases, to be one of special danger. Furthermore, when we go more deeply into the history of this case, we find that adolescence did not create any change in the style of life. Before that time the boy had been gradually losing hope of being the first in a life of social usefulness, and the more hopeless he grew, the more he had wandered into the easier ways of useless compensation.

This young man's earliest remembrance was : " I was running round the whole day in a kitty car." When he was cured he was taken back into his father's office, but he finally adapted himself to life as a travelling salesman.

Many first remembrances are concerned with situations of danger, and they are usually told by persons with whom the use of fears is an important factor in the style of life. A married woman once came to ask me why she was terrified whenever she passed a pharmacy. Some years previously she had spent a long time in a sanatorium undergoing treatment for tuberculosis, and a few months before I saw her a specialist had pronounced her cured, entirely healthy, and fit to have children. Shortly after this plenary absolution by the doctor she began to suffer from her obsession. The connection is obvious. The pharmacy was a warning reminder of her illness, an employment of the past to make the future ominous. She was connecting the possibility of a child with danger to her health. Though she and her husband had agreed that they wanted a child, her behaviour clearly showed her secret opposition. Her objection was stronger than any logical reasons, which latter the doctor as an expert could minimise, but he could not remove the symptom of fear. In this as in many similar cases we know in advance that the real reasons lie deeper, and are only to be found if we can discover the most important strivings in the style of life. Seldom, if ever, is it true that resistance to having children is based upon objective fears of childbirth or illness.   In this case it was easy to discover that the woman had been a pampered child who wanted to be in the centre of the stage.   Such women do not wish to bring a little rival on to the scene, and argue against it with every variety of reason and unreason.   This woman had trained herself perfectly in the expression of weakness and in perceiving opportunities to take the centre of attention.   Asked for her earliest recollection she said : " I was playing before our little house on the outskirts of the town, and my mother was terrified when she saw me jumping on the boards that covered the well."

A student of philosophy came to consult me about his erythrophobia.   From earliest childhood he had been teased because he blushed so easily, and for the past two months this had so much increased that he was afraid to go to a restaurant, to attend his lectures, or even to go out of his room.   I found that he was about to sit for an examination.   He was a faint-hearted man, timid and bashful, and whether he was visiting in society, working, or in company with a girl he suffered alike from acute tensions of feeling. Being a sympatheticotonic type,[1] this tension irritated the vegetative nervous system : his blushing had latterly worried him more, and he began to use it as a pretext for retreat.   From childhood this man had had a strong antipathy towards his mother, who was partial to his younger brother ; and he now no longer believed that he could achieve any success if he went on.   Here is his earliest remembrance : " When I was five years old I went out with

[1] An attempt has been made to describe two types of neurotics :—the vagotonic and the sympatheticotonic—according as one or other division of the vegetative nervous system with its associated glands tends to overact.   Sympatheticotonia is associated with increased metabolism.

my three-year-old brother. My parents were much excited when they found we had left the house, because there was a lake near by, and they were afraid that we had fallen into it. When we returned I was slapped." I understood this to mean that he did not like his home, where he felt that he was slighted, and this opinion was corroborated when he added, "I was slapped, but not my brother." But the discovery that he had been in a dangerous situation had no less impressed him, and this was reflected in his present behaviour, which was dominated by the notion—not to go out, not to venture too far. Such persons feel as though life were a trap; and it is easy to imagine this patient's painful experience when in contact with a girl, being teased and blushing, annoyed and annoying.

IX

Further Useless Goals of Superiority

THE loftiest goals are to be found in the most pathological cases—that is, in the psychoses. In cases of schizophrenia we often find the desire to be Jesus Christ. In manic-depressive cases also, in the manic phases, the patient frequently wishes to be the saviour of mankind, whilst in the depressive phases he often complains of being the greatest evil on earth. In paranoia the patient not only strives to be the centre of attention, but actually believes he is that already. Individual Psychology has shown that the goal of superiority can only be fixed at such altitudes when the individual has, by losing all interest in others, also lost interest in his own reason and understanding. Moreover the height of the goal now confronts the individual with such difficulties that common sense has become useless to him— incapable of solving them.

This goal of personal supremacy blocks the approach to reality. The more reality presents him with real, or even alluring possibilities of action, the greater is the effort which a maladjusted person will make to avoid it, because his *feeling* of supremacy is proportionately increased thereby. The end result, and logical culmination of such a life-line is, of course, total isolation in an asylum.

Perhaps the most audacious goals of superiority are found in cases of general paralysis, in which there is generally the most marked loss of social feeling and mental control. But all cases of Cæsarian madness exhibit the same goal of godlikeness with an absence of social feeling ; moreover— and this is consistent with all our findings—there is always a high degree of cowardice. Similarly, whenever we find a marked insensibility to the pains of others, or under-valuation of others' lives—as in murderers and certain other criminals—we can trace the preparation for their develop-ment : they do it by deliberately breaking through the limits of social feeling, impelled by cowardice to seek relief on the useless side of life. Every murderer is a coward intoxicated with the idea of being a hero. I believe that the true psychology of these tendencies ought to be explained to all mankind, and that such instruction would do much to prevent " crime waves." For criminals derive some incentive from the prevalent superstition that crime is at least courageous : whereas in truth even the most audacious crime is deeply motivated by fear.

The development of a criminal tendency has something in common with the fascination of useless sports ; the desire to break a record is sometimes apparent, and one of the greatest inducements to crime is the sense of overcoming the law and the police. This is a very considerable grati-fication upon the useless side, since the individual can give himself a feeling of having beaten the world single-handed. And as, according to certain statistics, about forty per cent. of all punishable crimes pass without the detection of the criminal, nearly every criminal has had the experience of committing a crime without being found out. The chance of making a long nose at the police is very alluring to a cowardly soul.

The goal of personal superiority is such that it invariably magnifies one of the three questions of life out of all proportion. We find that a person's ideal of success becomes unnaturally limited to social notoriety, to business success, or to sexual conquest. Thus we see the social careerist, fighting and jealous ; the business magnate, extending his interests at the expense of all others ; and the amorous intriguer, the would-be Don Juan. Each disturbs the harmony of his life by thus leaving many necessary demands unsatisfied, and then tries to compensate by still more frantic strivings in his narrowed sphere of action.

In the realm of sexual perversion we find the goal expressed in a purely fictitious form. This is especially evident in the sadistic type, by which I mean the type whose will to dominate is connected with sexual irritation. It was a notable advance in the understanding of the psychic structure of perversion when we could prove that the symptoms of masochistic cases are also governed by a personal goal of superiority. In the fantasies of masochists as well as in their actions, the egoistic tendency has been clearly diagnosed. The masochistic attitude signifies : " I am not governed by your power of attraction ; it is you who must do what I would have you do." Although the tendency which this implies is more fully expressed in sadism, the demands of the sadist are obviously harder for him to enforce than the masochist's " demand to be bullied.'' But we find individuals who exhibit a mixture of masochistic and sadistic behaviour.

I have found that the purpose of most masochistic subjects is to escape love and marriage, because they do not feel strong enough to risk a defeat. They will regard the avoidance of defeat, even through ignominious escape, exactly as if it were a goal of superiority. By means of their masochistic tendencies they are able to exclude all the really eligible members of the other sex. In the case of a man whom I cured of homosexuality, the patient went so far as to have a masochistic relation with a prostitute. By means of homosexuality he excluded *all* women, and in his periods of masochism he excluded all *worth-while* women.

Similarly, among girls who indulge in masochistic fantasies, we often note that the superior goal towards which they strive takes the form of celibacy. They can only imagine love and marriage as a torture, and this fantasy of celibacy is itself a gratification which is consistent with their masochistic tendencies. In masturbation, whether physical or mental, a certain consistency is always apparent : it is the sexual attitude which is appropriate to the isolated individual. Correctly interpreted, it is the wish to exclude sexual partnership. In such cases the patient will always tend to regard a partner as the author of his or her humiliation : and this idea, even though avoided in reality, will be expressed in fantasy.

One way of attaining superior-feelings is by the irritation of others. Parents or teachers, husbands or wives, as the case may be, will be more or less subtly exasperated until they burst into a rage, and begin to attack or punish. To many children this proof of their power over others is a great satisfaction, and they often desist when they have produced the desired reaction.   Still more anti-social is the goal of superiority through the injury of another.   In its service every trifle of evidence against another person will be collected with malicious valuation, such as difference in nationality, standard of living, advancing age in the case of women, and any unusual features such as red hair or prominent nose or teeth : upon all these disadvantages of another, real or imputed, the neurotic feeling of inferiority feeds voraciously, as if it could fill its own emptiness by the contemplation of yet greater vacuity elsewhere.   And by such activity, of course, feelings of inferiority may be induced in the person who is attacked.

The height of the goal is freely revealed in waking fantasies, where the desire to be the richest man, an emperor, or a pioneer finds imaginary gratification, always an image of supremacy in the subject's own line of life, whatever it may be.

The degree of social interest also finds expression in these imaginings. For instance, fantasies of saving life, of stopping runaway horses and rescuing the drowning indicate a more social tendency than images of torturing or being tortured. Common among children is the fantasy that they do not really belong to their parents. It indicates dissatisfaction with their own parents for some reason or other, and enables them to believe that they are the secret offspring of noble parents.   This particular tendency of the fantasy is evinced in mass-psychology, by the fact that in myths and legends the heroes are invariably the sons and daughters of gods or demi-gods, or at least, while no one knows it, they are of royal parentage and the heirs to great power and estates.

A DOUBLE REMOVE FROM REALITY

Day-dreams of a true sadistic or masochistic nature occur in which the dreamer participates only as an observer and not as an actor ; enjoying the sight of the power of the conqueror, or identifying his own feelings with the weaker person. This dreaming of vicarious satisfaction is, of course, a double remove from reality, and indicates a still greater lack of courage. Such was the case of a man of thirty-two who suffered from erythrophobia. He believed that people could not help looking at him wherever he went, and so he blushed continually. He was short, cross-eyed, and also suffered from lameness, one leg being shorter than the other. He had been spoiled by his mother, but his brothers and sisters had disliked and repressed him. Thus, when he went to school, he assumed a wrong attitude to his schoolmates, but tried to maintain his personal ascendancy by becoming an excellent gymnast. Even this achievement, however, did not maintain him sufficiently in the height of general attention, and he endeavoured to supplement it by exciting the compassion of others : when this also failed to satisfy him, he drew attention to himself by clowning and playing the fool. Finally, despairing of winning the high esteem he wanted, he gave up and tried to escape both from society and from love. Wherever he met people, in the street, in restaurants, or in theatres, he experienced acute mental tension, and, being a vaso-motor type, he expressed it by blushing and feeling afraid. At the same time he acquired a paranoid fear that every policeman was watching him as a suspected person. The effect of all these symptoms was to make him isolate himself to a great extent and only to carry on the lightest and most occasional occupations.

This man's day-dreams, which are the point of this narrative, were largely sexual fantasies. His sexual life was, naturally, one of masturbation, but in these fantasies his great distance from the solution of the sex-problem was expressed by visualising boys beating each other, whilst he himself was only a " smiling third."

As a last resort he tried to take to business, but again finding that he was not appreciated, he developed another paranoid fancy, that all his comrades conspired against him. He went from his office into a sanatorium, where he met a woman who showed great sympathy for him. Although up to this point he had retreated from every problem of life he now felt the urge to go forward in the matter of love. But the old feeling of hopelessness and lack of courage persisted. He had long ago fixed his position as an observer of the struggle of life, and now a situation had arisen which challenged this position. And so, one day, he shot himself.

THE BLOATED RED FROG

Red hair is sometimes taken as a sufficient basis for a feeling of inferiority, and the part it may play in building up a neurosis is illustrated in the following case. A man of forty-five complained of heart-trouble, which had been first diagnosed as organic and later as a neurotic disturbance. As a child he had been greatly pampered by his mother, and because of his efforts to rule over his comrades he had been unpopular with them, and they had always teased him about his " copper nob." He was too unsociable to make friends, but very successful in his school-work.

Later on, he was treated psycho-analytically for two years, and the doctor who treated him advised him to marry another of his patients. Naturally, with such a lack of social interest, he could not make a success of marriage. He tried to rule his wife in an absurd manner, and when she resisted him in any way he became very tense and his pulse increased to a hundred and fifty a minute.

Such heart troubles may often be observed as the result of swallowing air. This habit is also connected with asthma, stomach trouble, tympanites, and even pseudo-pregnancy. Usually the patient knows nothing about it, and my experience leads me to believe that it often takes place in sleep. It is to be suspected in cases of morning sickness and particularly in hysterical emesis. The air-swallowing habit is caused by a great psychic tension, due to exaggerated feelings of inadequacy. It is probably due to some tendency deeply laid in human nature since it so commonly appears in times of crisis, such as during an examination, and while courting.

Air-swallowing was the trouble in this case also. After the psychic mechanism of it had been explained to him, the man had a dream. He said : " I saw a red frog, bloated with air." It is interesting to see how easily the attention of a patient is diverted from the real coherence of the case. He treated this dream as if it were a mystery which he could not understand. I interpreted it to him, explaining to him that while he was asleep he perfectly understood what he was doing, and that his dream was a way of saying : " I am like that red frog, suffering from my abnormal colouring and trying to blow myself up into a bigger being than I am." In his criticism of my explanation, however, it was evident that the patient did not wish to understand.

THE MAN WHO WANTED TO MARRY HIS COUSIN

The masculine protest is often apparent in the loftiest goals of personal supremacy. A man of forty came to me in a state of nervous irritation because he felt impelled, as if in a fit of irresponsibility, to marry a cousin. Marriage with a near relative, either in reality or in fantasy, generally indicates fear of the opposite sex, for incest is opposed to common sense, which demands a courageous mixing of blood. Incestuous inclinations are to be traced to cowardice and a sense of social inadequacy. This patient had always resisted impulses towards love and marriage. He denied himself various gratifications, such as playgoing and eating meat—he had lately become a vegetarian—attached the highest importance to chastity, and became greatly disturbed if he had to do business with a lady client in his own office. He was an eldest son, who had resented his deposition by a younger brother, and had also felt that he was slighted and pushed into the background by his mother, for which reason he had leaned more towards his father. His criticism of his mother, and later on of all women, was very bitter. His earliest memory was this : " When I was four years old we moved. I met a strange woman near the new apartment whom I tried to push into a ditch." He also remembered that his feeling for his grandmother had been very hostile.

This man had now come to an age at which it was natural for him to marry, and he felt the urge to do so, but not in a normal way, so he sought a near relative as a sort of half-measure. At the same time his irresponsibility and sudden regret disclose something deeper in the whole arrangement. What he really wanted was to give himself a deep warning never again to approach a girl as long as he lived. So he staged this little warning interlude, in which, of course, I was cast for the part of the sage counsellor who was to tell him not to marry, and that his desire to do so was only a neurotic manifestation.

Jealousy is very often employed in order to establish a relation of superiority.   The jealous partner lays down rules for the behaviour of the other, and enforces them with reproaches and in terms of moral reprobation.   The person against whom such conduct is directed is thereby degraded from the position of a partner to that of a dishonourable servitor, which gives the jealous one a sense of relative superiority.   Jealousy is also found in connection with paranoia and alcoholism, where its use is fundamentally similar.   In either case an acute lack of self-confidence drives the patient to strive for superiority by the fictitious method of torturing the sexual partner.   It is not true, as it is often stated, that alcoholism causes impotence in these cases.   In these manifestations the alcoholism, the impotence and the jealousy are co-ordinated in the useless striving to compensate for the absence of social adjustment, courage, and self-confidence ; and, as a whole, they indicate a progressively egoistic attitude.

THE WOMAN WHO BECAME JEALOUS AT SIXTY

Paranoia of the truest type, originating late in life, sometimes yields cases of jealousy which is really a hallucination, created to compensate for the state of helplessness.   A case in point was that of a woman who had once been very wealthy and had had every luxury, but afterwards became very poor.   Her two married daughters supported her and her husband, and kept them in the luxury to which they had been accustomed.   She felt deserted, however, and unable to adapt herself to her new limitations, for she had been too much used to extravagance and power.   Her daughters, occupied with their families, paid her little attention, and all that was left to her was her husband, in whom she tried to find compensation for all that she had lost.   Naturally, it was impossible for him to accept such a position : nothing short of his entire obedience and servitude would have maintained the sense of personal superiority that she required, and his submission to her fell far short of her demands.   This intensified her already wounded dignity, and in the effort to enforce her ascendancy she accused her husband of unfaithfulness, although he was seventy years of age and she was sixty.   There was a young maid living in the house, and the wife interpreted her husband's kindness to this girl as a sign of intimacy. Thenceforth she fancied that every sound she heard in the house by day or night was a confirmation of her belief. The servant finally left and took a situation in another city, but the patient could not be convinced that she was not still in the neighbourhood, believed that she heard her knock at the door at night, and suspected that she was still communicating with her husband by advertisements in the newspapers.

It is not difficult to understand why she could not do without her jealousy.   Her husband's and her daughters' attitude towards her had changed since the time when she had lived in the focus of their attention.   She now despaired of reality, but she still had the same goal of supremacy : and this jealousy enabled her, by an attitude of accusation, still to keep the circumstances revolving around the question of her personal prerogative.

NEUROTIC HEART AND JEALOUSY

There are many cases, however, in which patients indulge in jealousy without for a moment admitting the fact to themselves.   This is probably because jealousy is itself felt to be an inferior feeling, and so conflicts with the conscious self-valuation.

A certain patient complained of pains in the heart which recurred from time to time, especially when she felt discontented. She had been married for nearly twenty years, and the marriage was supposed to be a very happy one. The husband was a kind man, although weak, they had an accomplished daughter as their only child, and were living in very good circumstances. For a year the patient had been suffering from these pains, which radiated from the breasts into both arms, and angina pectoris had been suspected. But as no organic symptoms could be discovered, and as the pains always occurred after a mental disturbance, the diagnosis of a neurosis (pseudo-angina) was justifiable. Some time before the appearance of these symptoms, she had had a peculiar feeling in the legs, as though they were tied and she was unable to move them. The later symptoms she described as very painful, lasting for several minutes and ending with emesis. Closer enquiry revealed the fact that the pains reached the throat from the sternal region, and were associated with frequent emesis, flatulence and occasional tympanites. Where we find such complications of symptoms I would always recommend the practitioner to look for ærophagia, a condition which, in the present case, I could observe while I spoke to the patient.

This patient had come to me from abroad, and after arriving in Vienna her husband left her to spend some time in Berlin. On the night of his departure she could not sleep, and when I asked her what thoughts passed through her mind while she lay awake, she answered : " I kept on figuring out how far my husband was from Berlin." This remark convinced me that the woman was constantly thinking where her husband was—and wondering what he was doing. The fact that her marriage was a fortunate one made it all the more likely that she kept a sharp look-out. Such conditions are a fertile ground for jealous fears, especially in the case of a woman so ambitious as this one proved to be.

After the second night she related the following dream : " Someone showed me a calf which was lame and unable to walk. This person commanded me to slaughter it." The inability to walk was reminiscent of some of her own symptoms, so it was justifiable to suppose that she identified herself with the calf. In this connection the slaughter of the calf represented suicide, probably in this case by cutting the throat, but there was more in the lameness. In this she helped me a great deal by telling me that a friend of her husband suffered from ankylosis of the knees as a result of gonorrheal arthritis.

FEAR OF SYPHILIS

How wounded jealousy may be used in the service of the neurotic goal is illustrated in the case of a man of thirty-eight who suffered from agoraphobia. He was fairly intelligent, but this weakness precluded both work and social relations. The neurosis followed a disappointment, when the girl to whom he was engaged became unfaithful to him. He was then advised to take a good situation in another part of the country so that he might forget his calamity, and he did so, but after a few days' work he had his first fit of anxiety, was scared to death, and hurried back to his mother, with whom he lived from that time until I saw him. He told me that for some days before the first fit of anxiety he had been thinking continually of syphilis and of how easily he could become infected with it. This must be understood as a self-preparation, by the appropriate meditation, to keep at a distance from all women and to live only under the care of his mother. His behaviour was that of a pampered child, readily taking to flight from the world, and only sure of safety with his mother. His earliest recollection was an epitome of his life-plan : " When I was four years old I was in a room with my mother ; and I remember looking out of the window and looking at people working in the street." This fragment of memory conveys his abnormal need of a sheltered position and his interest in watching (he was shortsighted) " how others work." To be with his mother and observe others working was his only idea of escape from tension and anxiety. When he was cured he started in business as an interior decorator.

SHIRKING THE MASCULINE ROLE

Early memories often furnish significant hints of the way in which the sexual attitude has been built up. This was well illustrated in the case of a pampered boy of fourteen with a very expectant attitude to life, a bad sport who made great difficulties in learning to swim, and was disinclined to work or to learn anything, especially mathematics. Mathematics is often the chief difficulty with this type, probably because it demands special power of independent application to work. He confessed to his mother, who was his best companion, that for some time he had been liable to feel sexual excitement at the sight of a man's muscles in the swimming bath or elsewhere. The earliest experience he could recall was of walking out with his mother, when people often said, looking at his fair and curly hair, " What a pretty girl ! " When he was asked if he would like to be a girl, however, he denied it emphatically. In his conscious opinion it was better to be a man than a woman, but since he really wanted to have everything more easily he instinctively shirked the necessary preparation for a masculine rôle, and his goal was to be wooed and to receive attention as though he had been a girl. This appeared possible because he was pretty to look at, but in all other ways success looked difficult and doubtful, so he took refuge in laziness or incapacity. Such a style of life, it must be clearly understood, actually gives the patient a sense of relative power or rulership. It goes with a great aversion to all situations which one is unable to dominate, so that we need not be surprised at this boy's exaggerated fear of thunderstorms. A thunderstorm is a supreme example of a thing which you cannot manage or control. With the lofty ambition of a second and youngest child, this boy's obvious defeats had made him incapable of conceiving an adequate success as a man : hence the attempt to form a homosexual goal, to govern passively by being loved and worshipped.

A GIRL WITH MASOCHISTIC FANTASIES

In many cases a fragment of the prototype is revealed, when in a dream, fantasy or early recollection, the patient discloses some notion of a high superiority. Thus, a girl of twenty once said to me : " I had an old and, of course, imaginary memory of having once been high up in a cloud." She had been a very pretty child, spoilt by her father, who had committed suicide when she was fourteen. As we know, to lean upon the father is always a second-best alternative and indicates discontent with the mother, so that as I expected the patient had a younger sister. She changed in appearance at the father's death, losing her good looks. The younger sister was now more attractive than herself, and the mother was expending all her care upon an elder brother who had been ill for some time, so this pampered girl was left with no one to spoil her, and she began to fight for attention, especially as her brother was hostile to her. About this time she experienced a nasty shock ; she was returning from school one day when she passed a man who exhibited himself, and she ran home screaming with fear.

Such experiences with exhibitionists occur much more often than is generally known. There are many men who are too cowardly to strive for a real solution of the life-problem of sex and who, looking for a relief or substitute, stop short at some partial manifestation of sexuality. If they are visual types, and their vision is not transferred to other objects, they become voyeurs or exhibitionists. Their cowardice is confirmed by the fact that they generally approach children.

My patient's shock from the exhibitionist marked the beginning of agoraphobia. We must recognise, however, that she was training herself to attain the foremost position along a non-sexual line of life as in the earlier relation with her father. The height of her ambition is indicated by the early recollection, and it had become still more neurotically exalted because the sister had surpassed and the brother had repressed her, as well as by her mother's neglect. Such a goal of personal superiority was in danger from love and marriage, and she was naturally trying to exclude these possibilities. She made the most of this first experience of actual sexuality in order to justify herself in an overt rejection of sexual life altogether. I found that she was training herself in this attitude by means of certain day-dreams which were calculated to intoxicate her with the same idea. In one of these which recurred very often, especially when she had a sexual feeling, she fancied that a man resembling her brother threw her down and spat upon her, upon which she experienced gratification.

It is my experience that such masochistic fantasies are very commonly indulged by girls, and if ever disclosed they are taken to indicate an inclination to be subdued, which is supposed to be a female characteristic. On the contrary, such a day-dream is a more or less complex fulfilment of a desire which is fundamentally quite simple but is the reverse of submissive—namely, the desire to exclude a realistic sexual objective with its possibilities of defeat and humiliation. We see the fantasy building up the day-dreamer's resistance to love at the same time as it gratifies the sensational need ; firstly, because to be satisfied in a fancy is to teach oneself, "It is not necessary to have a real relationship," and secondly because satisfaction mixed with the imagination of a defeat (in this case degradation by a brother who disliked her) teaches one to feel that a real experience would be highly objectionable. Thus the fantasy is an appropriate meditation like a sort of prayer, in which the individual soul trains itself, in the first respect, to lose interest in others, and in the second, ardently to desire escape from marriage. Where masochism is actually expressed in attempts to form masochistic relations the aim is fundamentally the same—to establish a great distance from normal behaviour and natural conditions.

Nothing, then, could be further from the truth than the idea that masochistic fancies indicate a desire for subjection. This patient of mine had been looking round to find someone whom she could rule, had fastened upon her younger sister to be her obedient slave, and had finally prevailed upon her to accompany her in everything. Her breakdown revealed her intolerance of the slightest real control over her : she was given a situation, and when her employer told her to write something at his dictation, she could not do it.

X

Occupational Choices, and Sleep Postures

THE earliest recollections, as we have seen, are often involved with ideas of danger, and they are no less frequently connected with deep impressions of illness and death. It is easy to understand how the first experiences of these events, especially if connected with danger and fear, may oppress a child with inferior feelings. In all probability none but human beings are conscious of the fact that death is in the destiny of life, and this consciousness alone is enough to give mankind a sense of being terribly overpowered by Nature. If a child experiences a brusque contact with death at an early age, the whole style of life may be largely moulded by that single impression. In such a case the importance of death to life is invariably over-valued, and we can often perceive how the child's actions and reactions are so directed as to find relief from this oppressive idea, or compensation for it. Children adopt various tricks in their struggle against death. Some take an ostrich's refuge, avoiding every possible reminder of the subject, some develop other anxieties which keep the real terror out of consciousness, and there are others, more actively disposed, who strive to protect and arm themselves, and to overcome death. In all of these the so-called instinct of self-preservation is more than normally evident.

There are two methods of fighting death with some certainty of victory. The first is to preserve the race, by producing and rearing children. In so struggling to conquer the destiny of the individual, the strongest instincts may be allies, and the mind's interest may be quickened towards society and the future of mankind. This common-sense compensation for the fear of death naturally involves the healthiest conceptions of love, and the exclusion of all perversions. The second method, suited to more individual ambitions, is to live so as to influence the life of the future. This has been the ruling motive of many great men, who have done enduring work in art and science, and it is a purpose most clearly visible in the lives of poets. Both in the procreation of the race and in the progress of its culture, a leading part is played by this psychic striving to conquer death.

The fact that the work of many poets and philosophers has been largely motivated by the desire to overcome death is shown by the power of death in their reflections. We see it in Horace's " Exegi monumentum aere perennius," and in Heine's " Nicht in Düsseldorf am Rhein will ich stehn auf taubem Stein." And Tolstoy writes : " If I do not know how to act in any situation, I imagine—What should I do if I were going to die to-morrow ? "

The early fear of death may provoke a striving rather worse than useless, even though efficient. I have already made passing reference to the case of a boy of fifteen who had been deeply impressed by the death of an older sister, and often talked about death. When I asked him what he wanted to be, I thought he would say, " A doctor." But he answered : " A grave-digger, because I don't want to be the one who is buried. I want to bury the others." And he did so, in his own way, for he became a merchant, a hard man of business who " buried " his competitors.

Quite another way of life is very commonly taken by children who have had some sharp experience of death. They form an early desire to become physicians, and to master all medical knowledge in order to survive. In a discussion which I once opened in a medical society, nearly everyone present recounted memories of the death, mortal danger, or illness of some member of the family. A professional psycho-analyst who was present objected to my interpretation of this similarity of their experiences, which I could relate to many other cases of the earliest memories of physicians ; he insisted that his own first recollection was of quite a different character. He remembered saying to his sick mother, when he was four years old, " Wait a little, and when I am grown up I will buy you all the best and most expensive medicines."

Failing all three of these compensations, the fear of death may find a religious relief by faith in the immortality of the soul. This may appear in complicated forms such as reincarnation, or more directly, as in spiritualism. The latter is founded upon the value of the assumption that the spirits of the dead can still move, act, and speak—a value which we must fully admit, in the absence of more realistic hopes of conquering mortality.

Not only in physicians, but in all workers, the choice of the occupation is foreshadowed by some dominant interest of the psychic prototype. The development of this interest into the concrete realisation of work is often a lengthy process of self-training in which we can see the same idea adapting itself successively to various material possibilities. Thus a great interest in playing with toy soldiers, which may be a preparation for military life, may also be the prelude to success as the director of a department store. To play at sewing with needle and thread need not reveal a future tailor ; it may just as well be the first step towards the career of a surgeon. Playing with dolls is the sign of an interest which may well develop into marriage and family life, and it may also be the sign of a future nurse or teacher.

Both marriage and occupation demand power of independent action, and readiness to accept the division of labour. These qualities cannot exist without a certain degree of social feeling and adaptation, and it is often at the time when the choice of an occupation becomes necessary that the lack of social adjustment appears. I believe that the attention of children should be drawn fairly early in their schooldays towards the question : " What do I want to do later in life, and why do I want it ? " The ideas which are thus elicited, taken together with their organic deficiencies or peculiarities, are our best help in the vocational guidance of pupils. We should not only look for the most highly-trained interest, but seek to understand its root in the psychic prototype. Wherever we find an ability it is the result of an interest in which the child has trained itself, stimulated by the totality of its circumstances. So clearly does this appear, that we are justified in believing that anyone could accomplish anything, given the right training and the correct method.

By the way in which the child thinks and behaves and by its characteristic perceptions, its interest is being specialised for its future occupation. The interest as a whole, however, is increased or decreased by its sense of the attainability of its goal of superiority. In the course of its development, the child will concretise its goal in various unattainable forms, which it must be able to abandon without any fundamental discouragement. Our task, therefore, is to support the child *in soul* and not in consciousness. The closer its social contact remains, the more common-sense conceptions of superiority will it develop.

A child's idea of superiority is, of course, very often influenced by desire to surpass the father in his occupation. Thus, if his father is a public-school teacher, a boy may want to be a don. As a rule we find that the more the choice of the profession changes, the more the child understands reality : but in each choice we can always detect the impulse towards domination, the determination to attain a goal of importance or of security, or at the least to escape difficulty or defeat. The child paints a new picture of its future action from time to time ; but always conditioned by the same prototype motive. When the actual choice of the profession has to be made the child is confronted by the reality which it has long been approaching, and that reality may come in circumstances either hostile or friendly to its own striving. The goal of the working life has now to be fixed, however, and the youth strikes his bargain with reality by taking up work in an individual manner. Whatever latitude of choice may present itself, he decides *how* he will confront this necessity for action in accordance with all the facts as he understands them. It is not to be expected that his conclusions are perfectly correct. More or less of an individual mistake is invariably involved in his choice. The conception of his function, in its ideal final form, is distorted by irrelevant factors. Money is one of these, which in our present civilisation has an altogether exaggerated importance. This final form may be obscured also by an interest in long life and health, security, or social ambition, or be warped by domineering and critical tendencies.

In discouraged children there is generally a doubtful or despairing attitude, and every struggle reveals movement towards escape from the necessity of a decision. Very often this is shown in the selection of various and inconsistent professions, preference for no profession at all, empty ideals, lack of adventure, or by delinquent tendencies.

It is well worth while to compare all the selections of a profession which a child makes in the course of its development, for, taken as a whole, they disclose the line of action and the degree of social interest and courage. We should not ignore the queerest and most fantastic choices, for they are related in a metaphorical way to the attitude a child is preparing to assume towards the demands of reality. One boy, for instance, when I asked what he wanted to be later in life, replied, " A horse." He was always trying to imitate both the movements and the speed of a horse. In his babyhood he had suffered from endocarditis and had been obliged to lie very still in bed for a long period. Later on he expressed his choice of a profession more realistically by becoming an automobile engineer. Another boy seven years old also symbolised his ambition by wanting to be a horse. When asked for the reason, he said, " My father is ill, and as I am the eldest I shall have to support the family."

In either of these cases it would be ridiculous to seek for the cause of the fantasy in phylogenetic influences or in sexual motives. The first boy was interested in movement, because the confinement of his illness had given him a specific feeling of inferiority. The second boy's use of the idea of the horse was entirely different. He was considering how best to replace and surpass his father, and the horse was the symbol of his future as the bearer of a heavy burden. I found another of these animal-fantasies in a boy of ten, who wanted to be a buffalo, and used to charge home from school in a posture imitative of an advancing bull. He developed into a bully : and his ideal character in history was Achilles.

The bodily postures and attitudes always indicate the manner in which an individual approaches his goal. A person who goes straight on shows courage, whereas an adult who is anxious and hesitant has a style of life that prohibits direct action, and something of a détour appears in every action. We can always detect by the way in which an individual gives his hand whether he has social feeling and likes to be connected with others. A perfectly normal handshake is rather rare ; it is usually overdone, underdone, or betrays a pushing-off or pulling-to tendency. It is noticeable in a tramcar that some people lean sideways ; they wish to be supported and are quite oblivious of others' convenience. The same social insensibility is seen in those who cough in front of others, quite thoughtless of infecting them. Some, in entering a room, seem to keep instinctively at the greatest possible distance from everyone else. All these things reveal, more directly than their conversation, the attitudes that individuals assume towards life.

The attitudes adopted in sleep are as significant as the postures and movements of daily life. Very little children sleep upon their backs, with the arms raised ; and when we see a child sleeping in this position we may assume that it is healthy. If the child changes this position and sleeps with the arms down, for example, some illness is to be suspected. Similarly, if an adult is accustomed to sleep in a certain position, and suddenly changes it, we may assume that something is altered in his mental attitude. Organic defects play their part, of course, in conditioning the sleeping posture. A person suffering from pneumonia or pleurisy will always sleep upon the defective side, sometimes without knowing why he does so. He does it unconsciously because it eases the breathing. Some persons who have heart trouble, or think they have, believe that they cannot sleep upon the left side. There is no organic reason for this, but they feel that they must be careful of the side which is the weaker.

When we see a person sleeping upon the back, stretched out like a soldier at attention, it is a sign that he wishes to appear as great as possible. One who lies curled up like a hedgehog with the sheet drawn over his head is not likely to be a striving or courageous character but is probably cowardly. We should be careful not to give him a difficult task until we have found out how to give him courage. A person who sleeps on his stomach betrays stubbornness and negativity.

By comparing the sleeping postures of patients in various hospitals with the reports of their daily life, I have concluded that the mental attitude is consistently expressed in both modes of life, sleeping and waking.

Some people turn a gradual somersault in sleep, and awake with their heads at the bottom of the bed and their feet on the bolster. Such people are psychically in an attitude of unusually strong opposition to the world, of the neurotic type which will often answer "No" before having understood the question. There are also patients who make a half-turn and sleep with their heads hanging down over the edge of the mattress. They develop headaches from this practice, which are generally used to escape the demands of the following day.

I was considerably puzzled by the discovery that some children sleep in a crouching position, resting on their knees and elbows like animals ; but I finally found out that this is the best position in which to hear what is happening in the next room. It is adopted by children who have more than the normal desire to keep in contact with others, even in sleep, and they generally want to go to bed with the door open.

Thus all postures have a purposive nature. I once treated a man who had become blind, and since then had always wanted to hold his wife's hand while he slept, which prevented her from moving. This was a pathetic disguise for a tyrannical tendency. When she resisted it he developed hallucinations at night, and imagined that burglars had caught her and carried her off. This hallucination was a development of the same line of action, to keep her in his power.

Restless sleepers, who keep moving all night, show that they are dissatisfied and want to be doing something more. It may also be a sign that they want to be watched by another person, usually by the mother. When children cry in sleep it is for the same reason, that they do not want to be alone but would like to ensure notice and protection. The quietest sleepers are those who are most settled in their attitude to the problems of life. Their lives being well organised by day they can use the night for its proper purpose of rest and recreation, and their sleep is generally free from dreaming.

XI

Organ Dialect and Dreams

In cases where the patient begins with a feeling that treatment will of itself endanger the goal of superiority it is often difficult to make a start. I had such a case in a married woman of twenty-five, who suffered from an anxiety-neurosis. At the first interview I asked her to take a chair beside me, and she went and sat down at the other side of the room.

Her violent attacks of anxiety occurred when her husband was delayed in coming home. She had felt curtailed in her life with her family, and her husband was the first person who had treated her with over-indulgence, but now his business obligations made it impossible for him to devote himself so much to her. She now wanted to be connected only with her husband and to exclude everyone else, and by the development of an anxiety-neurosis she was hindering her husband's business. No one else could demand anything from her, and her husband had to obey, but she paid for this success by very painful anxieties, and her husband had been able to persuade her to come and see me.

Not unnaturally, the situation was an *impasse*. She felt before coming that I was a danger to her, and symbolised her attitude in her behaviour over the chair. If I freed her from her neurosis she would have no weapon with which to face her husband.

AN OVERCRITICAL COMPULSIVE HOUSEWIFE

Another such case was that ot a married woman who had been the youngest of a very competitive family. She had been reproached and teased as the inferior member of the family, and as a girl had found no way of compensating for this unfortunate position, except to prove that other people were not in the right. This habit **won** her the nickname of " the judge."

When she married it was in order to get even with her married sisters. She was not in love with her husband, but was afraid of being despised if she did not prove herself capable of a happy marriage. But although she had three children she could never feel equal to others, so she defended herself against society by roughness, arrogance, and criticism. Such behaviour is often nothing but a neurotic safeguard against disappointment, and it is a complete misjudgment to call it the result of inherited psychopathic conditions.

She felt sure that she could not equal her eldest sister in the art of housekeeping, and her husband made a mistake when they were first married, by asking her if she would be as orderly as her sister. This touched her on the sensitive spot, and from that time onward she wanted to avoid housekeeping, or at least to fail in it under extenuating circumstances. A form of compulsion-neurosis ensued, which took the form of devoting herself to the linen and laundry work until her care and accuracy were a nuisance and a waste of time. As this left her no time for anything else she had an excuse if the marriage developed unhappily.

She had another device by which to defend herself which is not uncommonly used by neurotics ; she used to judge other people by their likeness or unlikeness to Jesus Christ. Thus, after setting anyone on a pedestal for admiration, it was easy for her to discover faults in him, to prove that he was not a Christ-like character, and then to cast him off. She used this defence against the many doctors to whom she went for treatment, and frustrated their efforts because of her prototypic feeling that if she were understood she would be " put back " to her inferior position of the youngest. She had, therefore, to prove the doctors wrong, always tried to forestall their opinions, and constantly worried and reproached, so that they were unable to speak, and the time of the consultations passed ineffectually.

––––––

As we have seen in a variety of cases, the organic functions are dominated by the style of life. This is notably the case with the lungs, the heart, the stomach, the organs of excretion and the sexual organs. The disturbance of these functions expresses the direction which an individual is taking to attain his goal. I have called these disturbances the organ dialect, or organ jargon, since the organs are revealing in their own most expressive language the intention of the individual totality.

The dialect of the sexual-organs is especially expressive and very often leads the patient to the doctor. Each case has its peculiarities, but in practically every one the patient is expressing by a disorder of the sexual functioning, a stoppage, hesitation, or escape in the face of the three life-problems. Whatever partial sexual satisfactions the patient may be providing for himself are of the nature of an escape from the real problem, and the remainder which is left over for a normal expression has to be excluded. In this way the various forms of impotence are traceable to a common root in a disinclination and lack of training for relations with other persons. This is always demonstrable when we leave the sexual symptoms temporarily out of account, and study the nature of the patient's social contacts. Most of the cases which I have known, of this specific functional failure, concerned patients faced with the problem of marriage. Ejaculatio præcox varies much in its individual meaning, but I have found it to be a sign of an egoistic character and a feeling of impotence, and it invariably goes with a very poor social adjustment. Failure to ejaculate occurs in egoistical men who are afraid of having children, generally because of their possible rivalry.

Nobody who has understood anything of Individual Psychology would attempt to cure such cases as these by upbraiding the patients with the words I have used, as if we could do good by taking up a moralistic attitude. A patient has to be brought into such a state of feeling that he likes to listen, and wants to understand. Only then can he be influenced to live what he has understood.

In women the same dialect appears as vaginismus. This is an avoidance of man, which is accompanied by other mental symptoms signifying the woman's aversion either to a certain man or to men in general. Besides this active avoidance there are the passive forms of sexual rejection, frigidity and a display of passivity. This lack of function mirrors an idea in the woman's mind of not being present in intercourse, as though the event were only the man's affair. In all cases of frigidity I have found that the woman felt the female rôle as one of humiliation and curtailment. It is important to verify this precisely and apart from the sexual life.

A GIRL'S REVENGE AGAINST HER FATHER

Ambitious girls who have been too much spoilt may easily lose confidence in regard to sexual relations. This was the case with a very beautiful girl whom I treated, the youngest of the family and spoiled by everyone, especially by the father until he married a second time. His re-marriage undermined her self-confidence. It is very difficult for a step-mother to take her place in relation to her husband's children without exciting their antagonism. I do not know if others have the same experience, but I have found that it is the girls who make the most trouble in these cases, and if an opportunity offers, they begin free sexual relations as if in revenge. When they are intelligent and sensitive enough to feel the full difficulty of the situation, they are conscious of a lack of love from both sides, and often become frigid and elude marriage, which was the case with my patient. We might well ask why this girl continued to enter into sexual relations at all, if we reckon up all that she had against it. She had the memory of being deserted by her father, the experience that a lover did not pamper her as her father did, and in addition to these things she had the gruesome experiences of undesired pregnancy and artificial abortion without physical gratification in love. To set against all these disadvantages she had nothing but a secret sense of being revenged upon her father

An individual can never settle down into such an unsatisfactory style of life, which excludes marriage and is ill-adapted to social relations or to work. What happens is a state of continual tension, which becomes acute in the face of every real problem that may present itself ; and which often appears in headache and fatigue.

My patient dreamed : " Jesus Christ appeared to me, and invited me to go to Heaven with Him, where my task would be to amuse all the other people   If I did not choose to do this I was to go to Hell.   Then I found myself in Heaven, and saw many angels who looked like the penguins in Anatole France's satire, and I also saw God, shaving His beard and looking and moving like the man in the advertisements in the chemist's shop-windows.   I felt a great despair and wanted to go away."

This dream is difficult to interpret unless we relate it to the general line of the girl's development ; indeed we should not make any sense of it if we could not estimate, from her history and its involved line of action, what was the emotional idea with which she was trying all the time to intoxicate herself.   This was an idea of rejecting virtue and taking to vice, motivated by revenge against the father, who wanted virtue of her.   Having grasped this fundamental agreement of the dream with everything else the patient is doing we can proceed to interpret : " To amuse the other people " corresponds to her notion of the humiliation of the female rôle, which she conceives as only an amusement for men.   Jesus Christ is her supreme symbol of a man of very earnest and unselfish character who proposed to marry her : He had said to her, " I want to sacrifice myself to make you happy."   Heaven, therefore, is the heaven He promised her in marriage.   But as we have seen, she is fearful of defeat in marriage, so that married life cannot be allowed to seem attractive, upon the same principle that the grapes which are too high to reach must be suspected of being sour.   So in her dream, this man in his little village appeared to her in the contemplative mood of the Viennese satirist, Nestroy, when he wrote :

" What is a man ? Getting up, shaving and going to sleep again ! "

DEPRESSION AS A SAFEGUARD AGAINST MARRIAGE

A much-spoiled girl, the youngest of eleven sisters and brothers, and correspondingly ambitious, had another way ot making the grapes of marriage sour. She had a few sexual intimacies, but only with married men. I am always suspicious if a girl begins with married men, because the difficulties are obviously so much greater, and an impracticable choice is not to be simply explained away by insisting upon the uncontrollable power of love. It was easy in this case, to find out that the patient had been intimidated by her pampered upbringing, and was especially nervous of the issue of marriage because two older sisters had been happily married and she feared she would fail to surpass them. She had always been conscious of this, but was not so well aware of what she was doing in her successive *liaisons*. If one of her lovers wanted to get a divorce and marry her, she left him—depressed and crying a little, of course, but always firm because of the poor wife, who was usually a personal friend of hers. The depression soon ceased with the beginning of another affair, but finally, after breaking off an intimacy in these circumstances, she went into a melancholy that lasted for months.

It was then that she came to me : she was thirty-six years old and living with a brother who was a widower and who pampered her very much. But in their first months together he had spoken of marrying again, and suggested that she should marry too. Faced with this undesirable prospect, and in the act of breaking off a relationship, her illness was a device to " kill two birds with one stone ! " It gave the brother a warning to take more care of her, and herself a lesson not to begin again with another man because of new and more dangerous consequences.

Sleeping is another kind of waking. We could, of course, be equally justified in saying that waking is a variant of sleeping, the truth being that in order to understand them, either psychologically or biologically, we must give up the idea that they are contradictory states. Biologically considered, sleep is only a partial cessation of the organism's contact with its environment, a lessening of its functional activity. In sleep our attention retains a certain amount of contact with reality through feeling, hearing, and thinking, but we exclude the greater part of the connections between them. We observe the limits of our movements in bed and do not fall out. We select some noises as important enough to awaken us and neglect others, and we can even wake ourselves up at stated hours. All these activities which sleep does not exclude are also carried on in the waking state, often hardly any more consciously.

Hypnotism is also a variety of waking, but it differs from sleep by excluding a different class of activities. The hypnotised subject excludes whatever the hypnotist wishes him to exclude, having first agreed (whether he admits it or not) to accept only the hypnotist's commands. Thus hypnotism may be called sleeping to order. Apart from hypnotism this sleeping to order is not uncommon, especially among children. Thus hypnotism is a proof of very great obedience. It is often regarded as a justifiable method of medical or psychic treatment, but Individual Psychologists naturally avoid it, knowing that the essence of successful treatment is an increased courage and self-control. A patient must prove these qualities by using them himself, not by abdicating control to another. The frequent failures which follow hypnotic methods of treatment are the patient's revenge for having been unexpectedly attacked by suggestion during the hypnosis.

There is nothing surprising in the fact that hypnosis can remove or mitigate certain symptoms, though without permanent benefit. I have already pointed out that the same is true of many suggestive methods, which the patient regards in a magical or semi-religious light, but these things do not of themselves teach a better adaptation to life. Thus they give transitory alleviations, and seem to be most effective in reducing the neurotic symptoms accompanying certain organic diseases, such as apoplexy, after-effects of syphilis and multiple sclerosis. As Ludwig Stein has shown, nearly all organic illnesses produce more symptoms than are necessary. These nervous complications are best treated by the method of Individual Psychology, which, though it cannot cure pneumonia or heart disease, may very much relieve these conditions by encouraging the patient.

Our distinctive method of dream-interpretation is founded upon this recognition of the unity of the waking and sleeping life. This is an advance upon the valuable discoveries of Lichtenberg and of Freud, that dreams always contain signs of vital problems which the dreamer never recognises in his waking life, discoveries which our work amply confirms. But the dream is not merely the substitutionary satisfaction of wishes unfulfilled in waking—especially not of Freud's "infantile sexual desires"—but it is a function of the entire style of life, more dynamically related to the future than to the past—a fact intuitively known in antiquity when dreams were regarded as prophetic and not as historical.   The dreamer is engaged in moulding his attitude and disposition to the coming events of his life, storing up a certain reserve of feeling and emotion which could not be acquired in the day-time by contact with reality and by logical thinking.   He thus accumulates a certain irrational force to sustain him in the pursuit of his own goal of superiority in the problems he anticipates, to solve them in his own way and against the demands of common sense.

In dreams, therefore, we never find any other tendencies or movements than those manifested in the style of the waking life when the latter is coherently grasped.   We cannot oppose " consciousness " to " unconsciousness " as if they were two antagonistic halves of an individual's existence.   The conscious life becomes unconscious as soon as we fail to understand it—and as soon as we understand an unconscious tendency it has already become conscious.

The dream strives to pave the way towards solving a problem by a metaphorical expression of it, and in itself it is a sign that the dreamer feels inadequate to solve it by common sense.   A *metaphorical* conception of one's situation is a way of *escape* from it, as it may be used to support almost any kind of practical action.   This is best exemplified in the dreams which create the feelings and emotions of success, as they produce a kind of intoxication which perfectly resists the logic of communal life.   Naturally the dreamer does not recognise his own metaphor for what it is.   If he understood it, it would be ineffective for its purpose.   It is essentially a self-deception, in the interest of his own individual goal.   We should expect, therefore, that the more the individual goal agrees with reality the less a person dreams, and we find that it is so

Very courageous people dream rarely, for they deal adequately with their situation in the day-time.

There are problematic cases, of course. An absence of dreams may prove later on to be only an absence of their contents, which are entirely forgotten so that only the emotion remains. That is but a further step in the self-deceptive process of which dreaming is one of the functions, and its purpose is to prevent the individual from getting insight into his dreams. Or the absence of dreams may be a sign that the patient has come to a point of rest in his neurosis and established a neurotic situation which he does not wish to change. Short dreams indicate that the present problems are such that the dreamer desires to find a " short cut " between them and the individual style of life. Dreams which are long or very complicated are dreamed by patients who are seeking excessive security in their lives, and they generally indicate hesitation and a desire on the part of the patient to postpone even his own self-deception in case it should not work out rightly. The style of life is best shown by dreams which are often repeated, or which have remained in the memory for many years.

The methods of self-deception which we use in dreams can be seen not only in the abuse of comparisons, metaphors and symbols, but also in a tendency to narrow or foreshorten a present problem until only a part of it is visible—a part which cannot be judged by the same standards as the whole. The urgent and necessary decision of a vital problem, for example, may be dreamed of in the form of an unimportant school-examination.

ANTAGONISM TO WIFE IN WAKING AND DREAMING

A case in which dreams played an important part was that of a man who had been married eight years and had two children, but was disappointed in his wife. His great complaint against her was that she did not take sufficient care of the children. The accentuation of the duty to the children in marriage is always the sign of a deeper-lying disagreement with the partner. Whether this man was right or wrong about his wife's neglect of the children, he used his criticism of it to express a deeper reproach, and held it as a stronghold against her. This was evident from other details of his behaviour, which showed that he worried about her management of matters other than the children, such as her housekeeping. The real source of his antagonism was his belief that she had not married him for love, and he found confirmation in the fact that his wife had been frigid. I have always found that long-continued frigidity offends the husband in the highest degree, and both partners become more or less irritated. In order to have a powerful proof of his wife's guilt, instead of the real and humiliating reason for his condemnation of her, he developed this exaggerated fear for the children, and subsequently came to me because of headaches and a distaste for work. He was not courageous enough to get a divorce or to seek another woman, having grown up with the feeling that in childhood he had been put back by his mother.

This man became very jealous and lost all faith in women. One night he dreamed, " I was in a battle in the streets of a city, and in the midst of the shooting and burning many women were thrown into the air as if by an explosion." He afterwards suffered much from pity in remembering this picture, until my treatment enabled him to understand it. It agreed with his attitude to his marriage-problem, for in this dream he gratified his rage by picturing a general extermination of women, which he was compelled to repudiate because he was not without social feeling and compassion. We can see how this pitying after-thought enabled him to maintain the daily attitude he assumed towards his wife—that he was not at all *angry* with her, but only *solicitous* for the children. I should analyse the structure of his dream as follows :—He selected some terrible pictures from his memories of the war—we call this, the selection of an adapted thought—and then *compared* the relations between the sexes to such warfare. In this way he minimised the whole problem of the sexes to a small part of it—a battle—leaving out all the more important factors. When he recovered from his fright, and when his self-deception and self-intoxication were explained and understood by him he became quieter and the headaches ceased, but he did not wish to be reconciled to his wife. He then had another dream : " The youngest of my three children got lost and could not be found." As we know he had only two children, but he was very frightened both in the dream and after awakening from it.

The line of reproach which this patient had always taken against his wife was the accusation of neglecting the children. So if he imagined a third child lost it was a warning not to have more children and thus increase the danger. By this détour he could avoid resuming relations with his wife. Again we see how the selection of an adapted thought enables him to work up a comparison which minimises the whole problem of educating and protecting children to one detail of it. Nevertheless, a very acute psychologist may detect, in the selection of the fiction of a *third* child, the beginning of a movement towards reconciliation. For it is as though the patient glimpsed the possibility of another, but withdrew, saying, " She may be careful enough for two, but surely not for three."

The self-deception practised in dreams is very often trace-able in the waking state, a fact of which I once had a very interesting proof. I was about to leave Vienna when a former patient rang me up and asked me to see his sick wife. He had consulted two physicians and neither could decide what was the course of the fever. I was in a hurry and tried to excuse myself, saying that I was not a specialist in organic illnesses, but I finally yielded to his insistence. I found the patient was suffering from typhus, and recom-mended a consultant who was skilful in such cases He still resisted, saying that no physician could tell him more than I could, and I had difficulty in getting away with a promise that I would visit him as a friend as soon as I returned to Vienna. He kept on saying " But he could not tell me more than you have told me." At last I persuaded him to call in the expert, and went away. When I returned to visit him a few weeks later his wife was recovering, and he told me he was very well satisfied with the doctor I had recom-mended. Then, in a very positive tone, he observed, " Of course, you told me when you came that Dr. W. had died that morning."

I had told him nothing of the kind, so I denied it. I had only read the news myself in my vacation the day after leaving Vienna. He would not believe this, however, and stoutly maintained that I had spoken of Dr. W.'s death. When I asked him what made him think I had told him, he answered, " Why, you must have done so. For when the consultant came to see my wife the next day, he had no sooner greeted everyone present than he turned to the doctors and said, ' Do you know my friend, Dr. W., is dead?' ' Yes,' I interposed, ' Dr. Adler told me so yesterday.' The specialist looked surprised and said, ' I know Dr. Adler very well, but I did not know he was blessed with the gift of prophecy.' There must be some mistake, and I wonder if you can explain it."

It was not so difficult to explain. This man had almost unlimited faith in me, and when I saw him before my departure he had repeatedly said, "The specialist cannot tell me anything that you haven't said." He had intoxicated himself with this idea, so that he received the new doctor with an emotional determination that whatever he said, it would be something I had already told him. Thus he spontaneously took the first piece of information which the specialist uttered and firmly, and with perfect self-deception, ascribed it to me.

Bibliography

Revised, 1967, by Heinz L. Ansbacher

Books by Alfred Adler in English.

Those currently in print in the United States are marked with asterisk (*).

Study of organ inferiority and its psychical compensation: a contribution to clinical medicine (1907). Trans. S. E. Jelliffe. New York: Nervous and Mental Disease Publ. Co., 1917. Pp. x + 86.

The neurotic constitution: outline of a comparative individualistic psychology and psychotherapy (1912). Trans. B. Glueck and J. E. Lind. New York: Moffat, Yard, 1917. Pp. xxiii + 456. Adler's fundamental psychological work; not easily readable.

The practice and theory of Individual Psychology (1920). Trans. P. Radin. Paterson, N. J.: Littlefield, Adams, 1959. Pp. viii + 352. Paper. Important collection of 28 papers published during 1909–1920.

Understanding human nature (1927). Trans. W. B. Wolfe. New York: Premier Books, 1957. Pp. 224. Paper. Based on lectures before an adult education audience.

The case of Miss R.: the interpretation of a life story (1928). Trans. Eleanore and F. Jensen. New York: Greenberg, 1929. Pp. xxii + 306.

* *Problems of neurosis; a book of case histories* (1929). P. Mairet, ed., Intro. by H. L. Ansbacher. New York: Harper Torchbooks, 1964. Pp. xxvi + 180. Paper. While presenting some 37 cases, manages to cover the salient features in the Adlerian system of theory and therapy.

The science of living. Preface by P. Mairet. New York: Greenberg, 1929. Pp. 264. Includes particularly chapters on style of life, inferiority and superiority complexes, early recollections, and dreams.

The education of children. Trans. Eleanore and F. Jensen. New York: Greenberg, 1930. Pp. 309. Includes family position, school problems, adolescence, educating the parents.

The pattern of life. Ed. W. B. Wolfe. New York: Cosmopolitan Books, 1930. Pp. 273. Twelve cases brought to Adler's clinic at the New School for Social Research, New York, during his 1929 lecture season.

The problem child: the life style of the difficult child as analyzed in specific cases (1930). Trans. from the French by G. Daniels. Introd. K. A. Adler. New York: Capricorn Books, 1963. Pp. xvii + 172. Paper. Interviews with 22 children, their parents and teachers, and case analyses.

What life should mean to you (1931). Ed. A. Porter. New York: Capricorn Books, 1958. Pp. 300. Paper. A good general introduction with chapters on the meaning of life, mind and body, and crime and its prevention, among others.

* *Social interest: a challenge to mankind* (1933). Trans. J. Linton and R. Vaughan. New York: Capricorn Books, 1964. Pp. 313. Paper. Adler's last and most advanced presentation of his views.

* *The Individual Psychology of Alfred Adler: a systematic presentation in selections from his writings.* Eds. H. L. and Rowena R. Ansbacher. New York: Basic Books, 1956; Harper Torchbooks, 1964. Pp. xxiii + 503. "Should be the equivalent of a textbook by Adler."

* *Superiority and social interest: a collection of later writings.* Eds. H. L. and Rowena R. Ansbacher. Evanston, Ill.: Northwestern University Press, 1964. Pp. xxi + 432. Of the 21 selections, 9 are here translated for the first time. Includes Adler's essay on religion, a biography and a virtually complete bibliography of his writings.

Biographies of Adler

Bottome, Phyllis. *Alfred Adler: a portrait from life.* New York: Vanguard, 1957.

Furtmüller, C. Alfred Adler: a biographical essay. In A. Adler, *Superiority and social interest.* Evanston, Ill.: Northwestern University Press, 1964. Pp. 311–393.

Orgler, Hertha. *Alfred Adler: the man and his work.* New York: Liveright, 1963; Capricorn Books, 1965. Paper.

Pertinent Contemporary Books by Others

Adler, Alexandra. *Guiding human misfits.* New York: Philosophical Library, 1948.

Adler, K. A., and Deutsch, Danica (Eds.) *Essays in Individual Psychology: contemporary application of Alfred Adler's theories.* New York: Grove Press, 1959. Paper.

Beecher, Marguerite and W. *Parents on the run.* New York: Julian Press, 1955. Agora Softback. 1966. Paper.

Beecher, W. and Marguerite. *Beyond success and failure: ways to self-reliance and maturity.* New York: Julian Press, 1966.

Brachfeld, O. *Inferiority feelings in the individual and the group.* New York: Grune & Stratton, 1951.

Dinkmeyer, D., and Dreikurs, R. *Encouraging children to learn: the encouragement process.* Englewood Cliffs, N. J.: Prentice-Hall, 1963.

Dreikurs, R. *The challenge of parenthood.* New York: Duell, Sloan & Pearce, 1948.

Dreikurs, R. *Psychology in the classroom.* New York: Harper & Brothers, 1957.

Dreikurs, R. *Children: the challenge.* New York: Duell, Sloan & Pearce, 1964.

Dreikurs, R., Corsini, R. J., Lowe, R., & Sonstegard, M. *Adlerian family counseling: a manual for counseling centers.* Eugene, Oregon: University of Oregon Press, 1959. Paper.

Ganz, Madelaine. *The psychology of Alfred Adler and the development of the child.* New York: Humanities Press, 1953.

Gondor, E. I. *Art and play therapy.* New York: Random House, 1958. Paper.

Ray, Marie B. *The importance of feeling inferior.* New York: Harper & Brothers, 1957.

Way, L. *Adler's place in psychology: an exposition of Individual Psychology.* New York: Collier Books, 1962. Paper.

Textbook Chapters on Adler

Bischof, L. J. *Interpretating personality theories.* New York: Harper & Row, 1964. "Adler," pp. 231–266.

Farberow, N. L., & Shneidman, E. S. (Eds.) *The cry for help.* New York: McGraw-Hill, 1961. Paper. *"Suicide: The Adlerian point of view"* by H. L. Ansbacher, pp. 204–219.

Ford, D. H., & Urban, H. B. *Systems of psychotherapy.* New York: Wiley & Sons, 1963. "Alfred Adler's subjectivistic system of Individual Psychology," pp. 304–365.

Hall, C. S. & Lindzey, G. *Theories of personality.* New York: Wiley & Sons, 1957. "Social psychological theories: Adler, Fromm, Horney, and Sullivan," pp. 114–156.

Munroe, Ruth L. *Schools of psychoanalytic thought.* New York: Dryden Press, 1955. "Adler, Horney, Fromm, and Sullivan," pp. 333–536.

Stein, M. I. (Ed.) *Contemporary psychotherapies.* New York: Free Press of Glencoe, 1961. "The Adlerian approach to psychodynamics and to therapy," by R. Dreikurs, pp. 60–94.

Wepman, J. M. & Heine, R. W. (Eds.) *Concepts of personality.* Chicago: Aldine Publishing Co., 1963. "Individual Psychology: the Alderian point of view" by R. Dreikurs, pp. 234–256.

Wolmann, B. B. *Contemporary theories and systems in psychology,* New York: Harper & Brothers, 1960. "Alfred Adler: Individual Psychology," pp. 283–298.

Wolmann, B. B. & Nagel E. (Eds.) *Scientific psychology: principles and approaches.* New York: Basic Books, 1965. "The structure of Individual Psychology" by H. L. Ansbacher, pp. 340–364.

Woodworth, R. S., & Sheehan, Mary R. *Contemporary schools of psychology.* (3rd ed.) New York: Ronald Press, 1964. "Alfred Adler and the school of 'Individual Psychology,' " pp. 297–305.

Journal

Journal of Individual Psychology. Published by the American Society of Adlerian Psychology. H. L. Ansbacher. Editor, University of Vermont, Burlington, Vermont.

INDEX

ACHILLES, 118, 151
Adopted child, situation of the, 22
Aerophagia (air-swallowing), 94, 95, 135, 139
Aggression, truth as weapon of, 24
Agoraphobia, 6, 11, 30, 92, 94, 95, 113, 140, 143
Alcoholism (see Drunkenness), 137
" All or nothing," neurotic formula, 55
Ambition, 22, 39, 42, 58, 59, 62, 84, 142, 158, 160
Ambivalence refuted, 87
Anamnesis, 118
Anger, and fainting, 51
——, and headaches, 58, 59
——, and masculine protest, 43
——, suppression of, 22, 60
——, use of, 29, 90, 91
Angina pectoris, 139
Animal characteristics and the prototype, 55, 116, 150, 151, 152, 153 (animal fantasies, 150, 151)
Ankylosis of the knees, 140
Antagonism, in marriage, 165, 166
—— to family, 97, 116, 127
—— to society, 99, 152, 155
Anxiety, and stomach trouble, 57
——, fictitious form of, 10
——, use of, 29, 84, 91, 122, 165
Anxiety neurosis, 2, 6, 11, 108–111, 139–140, 154
Apoplexy, 162
Appreciation, neurotic striving for, 11
Art, human value of, 78
Arthritis, gonorrheal, 140
Asthma, 97, 135
Astigmatism, 123
Athletics, as denial of femininity, 43, 45
Attachment to one parent, 92–93, 98, 111, 112, 142
Audacity, 118

BACKWARD child, 89
Beethoven, 35, 66
Begging attitude, 86–89, 108
Behaviour, changes in, 98
——, in love and society, 48
——, insulting, 116
——, not hereditary, 105
—— pattern, 19, 36, 37, 39, 42, 51, 75, 89, 105, 117
Beliefs, consequences of real, 62
Benjamin, 107
Biblical history, examples from, 105, 107, 108
Birth control, 111
Blushing, 126, 127, 133
Brain and blood circulation, peculiarities of, 51
" Brothers Karamazov, The," 106
Buzzing in the ears, 86

CAESARIAN madness, 129
Cancer, fear of, 108, 109
Castration complex, 67
Catatonia, 15
Celibacy, as goal of superiority, 131
Character, basic, relatively unchangeable, 30, 31
Charity, spurious, 37
Charlemagne, 4, 5
Child-bearing, attitudes to, 60, 61, 125
Children of great men, 5
Chorea, hysterical, 97
Civilisation, masculine rôle in, 24, 44, 66, 67
——, money over-valued in, 149, 150
——, over-intellectualised, 78
——, right-handed, 66
" Clairvoyance," neurotic's belief in his, 70
Cleaning mania, 12, 104
Clumsiness, 55, 64

harper ✦ torchbooks

HUMANITIES AND SOCIAL SCIENCES

American Studies: General

THOMAS C. COCHRAN: The Inner Revolution. *Essays on the Social Sciences in History* TB/1140

HENRY STEELE COMMAGER, Ed.: The Struggle for Racial Equality TB/1300

EDWARD S. CORWIN: American Constitutional History. *Essays edited by Alpheus T. Mason and Gerald Garvey* △ TB/1136

CARL N. DEGLER, Ed.: Pivotal Interpretations of American History TB/1240, TB/1241

A. HUNTER DUPREE: Science in the Federal Government: *A History of Policies and Activities to 1940* TB/573

A. S. EISENSTADT, Ed.: The Craft of American History: *Recent Essays in American Historical Writing* Vol. I TB/1255; Vol. II TB/1256

CHARLOTTE P. GILMAN: Women and Economics: *A Study of the Economic Relation between Men and Women as a Factor in Social Evolution.* ‡ *Ed. with an Introduction by Carl N. Degler* TB/3073

OSCAR HANDLIN, Ed.: This Was America: *As Recorded by European Travelers in the Eighteenth, Nineteenth and Twentieth Centuries. Illus.* TB/1119

MARCUS LEE HANSEN: The Atlantic Migration: 1607-1860. *Edited by Arthur M. Schlesinger* TB/1052

MARCUS LEE HANSEN: The Immigrant in American History. TB/1120

JOHN HIGHAM, Ed.: The Reconstruction of American History △ TB/1068

ROBERT H. JACKSON: The Supreme Court in the American System of Government TB/1106

JOHN F. KENNEDY: A Nation of Immigrants. △ *Illus.* TB/1118

LEONARD W. LEVY, Ed.: American Constitutional Law: *Historical Essays* TB/1285

LEONARD W. LEVY, Ed.: Judicial Review and the Supreme Court TB/1296

LEONARD W. LEVY: The Law of the Commonwealth and Chief Justice Shaw TB/1309

RALPH BARTON PERRY: Puritanism and Democracy TB/1138

ARNOLD ROSE: The Negro in America TB/3048

MAURICE R. STEIN: The Eclipse of Community. *An Interpretation of American Studies* TB/1128

W. LLOYD WARNER and Associates: Democracy in Jonesville: *A Study in Quality and Inequality* ¶ TB/1129

W. LLOYD WARNER: Social Class in America: *The Evaluation of Status* TB/1013

American Studies: Colonial

BERNARD BAILYN, Ed.: Apologia of Robert Keayne: *Self-Portrait of a Puritan Merchant* TB/1201

BERNARD BAILYN: The New England Merchants in the Seventeenth Century TB/1149

JOSEPH CHARLES: The Origins of the American Party System TB/1049

CHARLES GIBSON: Spain in America † TB/3077

LAWRENCE HENRY GIPSON: The Coming of the Revolution: 1763-1775. † *Illus.* TB/3007

LEONARD W. LEVY: Freedom of Speech and Press in Early American History: *Legacy of Suppression* TB/1109

PERRY MILLER: Errand Into the Wilderness TB/1139

PERRY MILLER & T. H. JOHNSON, Eds.: The Puritans: *A Sourcebook of Their Writings* Vol. I TB/1093; Vol. II TB/1094

EDMUND S. MORGAN, Ed.: The Diary of Michael Wigglesworth, 1653-1657: *The Conscience of a Puritan* TB/1228

EDMUND S. MORGAN: The Puritan Family: *Religion and Domestic Relations in Seventeenth-Century New England* TB/1227

RICHARD B. MORRIS: Government and Labor in Early America TB/1244

KENNETH B. MURDOCK: Literature and Theology in Colonial New England TB/99

WALLACE NOTESTEIN: The English People on the Eve of Colonization: 1603-1630. † *Illus.* TB/3006

JOHN P. ROCHE: Origins of American Political Thought: *Selected Readings* TB/1301

JOHN SMITH: Captain John Smith's America: *Selections from His Writings. Ed. with Intro. by John Lankford* TB/3078

LOUIS B. WRIGHT: The Cultural Life of the American Colonies: 1607-1763. † *Illus.* TB/3005

American Studies: From the Revolution to 1860

JOHN R. ALDEN: The American Revolution: 1775-1783. † *Illus.* TB/3011

MAX BELOFF, Ed.: The Debate on the American Revolution, 1761-1783: *A Sourcebook* △ TB/1225

RAY A. BILLINGTON: The Far Western Frontier: 1830-1860. † *Illus.* TB/3012

EDMUND BURKE: On the American Revolution: *Selected Speeches and Letters.* ‡ *Edited by Elliott Robert Barkan* TB/3068

WHITNEY R. CROSS: The Burned-Over District: *The Social and Intellectual History of Enthusiastic Religion in Western New York, 1800-1850* △ TB/1242

GEORGE DANGERFIELD: The Awakening of American Nationalism: 1815-1828. † *Illus.* TB/3061

CLEMENT EATON: The Freedom-of-Thought Struggle in the Old South. *Revised and Enlarged. Illus.* TB/1150

CLEMENT EATON: The Growth of Southern Civilization: 1790-1860. † *Illus.* TB/3040

---

† The New American Nation Series, edited by Henry Steele Commager and Richard B. Morris.
‡ American Perspectives series, edited by Bernard Wishy and William E. Leuchtenburg.
* The Rise of Modern Europe series, edited by William L. Langer.
** History of Europe series, edited by J. H. Plumb.
¶ Researches in the Social, Cultural and Behavioral Sciences, edited by Benjamin Nelson.
§ The Library of Religion and Culture, edited by Benjamin Nelson.
Σ Harper Modern Science Series, edited by James R. Newman.
° Not for sale in Canada.
△ Not for sale in the U. K.

EDWARD BURNETT TYLOR: The Origins of Culture. *Part I of "Primitive Culture."* § *Intro. by Paul Radin* TB/33
EDWARD BURNETT TYLOR: Religion in Primitive Culture. *Part II of "Primitive Culture."* § *Intro. by Paul Radin* TB/34
W. LLOYD WARNER: A Black Civilization: *A Study of an Australian Tribe.* ¶ *Illus.* TB/3056

Art and Art History

WALTER LOWRIE: Art in the Early Church. *Revised Edition. 452 illus.* TB/124
EMILE MÂLE: The Gothic Image: *Religious Art in France of the Thirteenth Century.* § △ *190 illus.* TB/44
MILLARD MEISS: Painting in Florence and Siena after the Black Death: *The Arts, Religion and Society in the Mid-Fourteenth Century. 169 illus.* TB/1148
ERICH NEUMANN: The Archetypal World of Henry Moore. △ *107 illus.* TB/2020
DORA & ERWIN PANOFSKY : Pandora's Box: *The Changing Aspects of a Mythical Symbol. Revised Edition. Illus.* TB/2021
ERWIN PANOFSKY: Studies in Iconology: *Humanistic Themes in the Art of the Renaissance.* △ *180 illustrations* TB/1077
ALEXANDRE PIANKOFF: The Shrines of Tut-Ankh-Amon. *Edited by N. Rambova. 117 illus.* TB/2011
JEAN SEZNEC: The Survival of the Pagan Gods: *The Mythological Tradition and Its Place in Renaissance Humanism and Art.* TB/2004
OTTO VON SIMSON: The Gothic Cathedral: *Origins of Gothic Architecture and the Medieval Concept of Order.* △ *58 illus.* TB/2018
HEINRICH ZIMMER: Myth and Symbols in Indian Art and Civilization. *70 illustrations* TB/2005

Business, Economics & Economic History

REINHARD BENDIX: Work and Authority in Industry: *Ideologies of Management in the Course of Industrialization* TB/3035
GILBERT BURCK & EDITORS OF FORTUNE: The Computer Age: *And Its Potential for Management* TB/1179
THOMAS C. COCHRAN: The American Business System: *A Historical Perspective, 1900-1955* TB/1080
THOMAS C. COCHRAN: The Inner Revolution: *Essays on the Social Sciences in History* △ TB/1140
THOMAS C. COCHRAN & WILLIAM MILLER: The Age of Enterprise: *A Social History of Industrial America* TB/1054
ROBERT DAHL & CHARLES E. LINDBLOM: Politics, Economics, and Welfare: *Planning and Politico-Economic Systems Resolved into Basic Social Processes* TB/3037
PETER F. DRUCKER: The New Society: *The Anatomy of Industrial Order* △ TB/1082
EDITORS OF FORTUNE: America in the Sixties: *The Economy and the Society* TB/1015
ROBERT L. HEILBRONER: The Great Ascent: *The Struggle for Economic Development in Our Time* TB/3030
ROBERT L. HEILBRONER: The Limits of American Capitalism TB/1305
FRANK H. KNIGHT: The Economic Organization TB/1214
FRANK H. KNIGHT: Risk, Uncertainty and Profit TB/1215
ABBA P. LERNER: Everybody's Business: *Current Assumptions in Economics and Public Policy* TB/3051
ROBERT GREEN MC CLOSKEY: American Conservatism in the Age of Enterprise, 1865-1910 △ TB/1137
PAUL MANTOUX: The Industrial Revolution in the Eighteenth Century: *The Beginnings of the Modern Factory System in England* ○ △ TB/1079
WILLIAM MILLER, Ed.: Men in Business: *Essays on the Historical Role of the Entrepreneur* TB/1081
RICHARD B. MORRIS: Government and Labor in Early America △ TB/1244
HERBERT SIMON: The Shape of Automation: *For Men and Management* TB/1245

PERRIN STRYKER: The Character of the Executive: *Eleven Studies in Managerial Qualities* TB/1041
PIERRE URI: Partnership for Progress: *A Program for Transatlantic Action* TB/3036

Education

JACQUES BARZUN: The House of Intellect △ TB/1051
RICHARD M. JONES, Ed.: Contemporary Educational Psychology: *Selected Readings* TB/1292
CLARK KERR: The Uses of the University TB/1264
JOHN U. NEF: Cultural Foundations of Industrial Civilization △ TB/1024
NATHAN M. PUSEY: The Age of the Scholar: *Observations on Education in a Troubled Decade* TB/1157
PAUL VALÉRY: The Outlook for Intelligence △ TB/2016

Historiography & Philosophy of History

JACOB BURCKHARDT: On History and Historians. △ *Introduction by H. R. Trevor-Roper* TB/1216
WILHELM DILTHEY: Pattern and Meaning in History: *Thoughts on History and Society.* ○ △ *Edited with an Introduction by H. P. Rickman* TB/1075
J. H. HEXTER: Reappraisals in History: *New Views on History & Society in Early Modern Europe* △ TB/1100
H. STUART HUGHES: History as Art and as Science: *Twin Vistas on the Past* TB/1207
RAYMOND KLIBANSKY & H. J. PATON, Eds.: Philosophy and History: *The Ernst Cassirer Festschrift. Illus.* TB/1115
ARNALDO MOMIGLIANO: Studies in Historiography ○ △ TB/1288
GEORGE H. NADEL, Ed.: Studies in the Philosophy of History: *Selected Essays from History and Theory* TB/1208
JOSE ORTEGA Y GASSET: The Modern Theme. *Introduction by Jose Ferrater Mora* TB/1038
KARL R. POPPER: The Open Society and Its Enemies △
 Vol. I: *The Spell of Plato* TB/1101
 Vol. II: *The High Tide of Prophecy: Hegel, Marx and the Aftermath* TB/1102
KARL R. POPPER: The Poverty of Historicism ○ △ TB/1126
G. J. RENIER: History: *Its Purpose and Method* △ TB/1209
W. H. WALSH: Philosophy of History: *An Introduction* △ TB/1020

History: General

L. CARRINGTON GOODRICH: A Short History of the Chinese People. △ *Illus.* TB/3015
DAN N. JACOBS & HANS H. BAERWALD: Chinese Communism: *Selected Documents* TB/3031
BERNARD LEWIS: The Arabs in History △ TB/1029
BERNARD LEWIS: The Middle East and the West ○ △ TB/1274

History: Ancient

A. ANDREWES: The Greek Tyrants △ TB/1103
ADOLF ERMAN, Ed. The Ancient Egyptians: *A Sourcebook of Their Writings. New material and Introduction by William Kelly Simpson* TB/1233
MICHAEL GRANT: Ancient History ○ △ TB/1190
SAMUEL NOAH KRAMER: Sumerian Mythology △ TB/1055
NAPHTALI LEWIS & MEYER REINHOLD, Eds.: Roman Civilization. *Sourcebook I: The Republic* TB/1231
NAPHTALI LEWIS & MEYER REINHOLD, Eds.: Roman Civilization. *Sourcebook II: The Empire* TB/1232

History: Medieval

P. BOISSONNADE: Life and Work in Medieval Europe: *The Evolution of the Medieval Economy, the 5th to the 15th Century.* ○ △ *Preface by Lynn White, Jr.* TB/1141
HELEN CAM: England before Elizabeth △ TB/1026
NORMAN COHN: The Pursuit of the Millennium: *Revolutionary Messianism in Medieval and Reformation Europe* △ TB/1037

G. G. COULTON: Medieval Village, Manor, and Monastery
TB/1022

CHRISTOPHER DAWSON, Ed.: Mission to Asia: *Narratives and Letters of the Franciscan Missionaries in Mongolia and China in the 13th and 14 Centuries* △
TB/315

HEINRICH FICHTENAU: The Carolingian Empire: *The Age of Charlemagne* △
TB/1142

GALBERT OF BRUGES: The Murder of Charles the Good. *Trans. with Intro. by James Bruce Ross*
TB/1311

F. L. GANSHOF: Feudalism △
TB/1058

DENO GEANAKOPLOS: Byzantine East and Latin West: *Two Worlds of Christendom in the Middle Ages and Renaissance*
TB/1265

EDWARD GIBBON: The Triumph of Christendom in the Roman Empire *(Chaps. XV-XX of "Decline and Fall," J. B. Bury edition).* § △ *Illus.*
TB/46

W. O. HASSALL, Ed.: Medieval England: *As Viewed by Contemporaries* △
TB/1205

DENYS HAY: Europe: The Emergence of an Idea
TB/1275

DENYS HAY: The Medieval Centuries ○ △
TB/1192

J. M. HUSSEY: The Byzantine World △
TB/1057

ROBERT LATOUCHE: The Birth of Western Economy: *Economic Aspects of the Dark Ages.* ○ △ *Intro. by Philip Grierson*
TB/1290

FERDINAND LOT: The End of the Ancient World and the Beginnings of the Middle Ages. *Introduction by Glanville Downey*
TB/1044

MARSILIUS OF PADUA: The Defender of the Peace. *Trans. with Intro. by Alan Gewirth*
TB/1310

G. MOLLAT: The Popes at Avignon: 1305-1378 △
TB/308

CHARLES PETIT-DUTAILLIS: The Feudal Monarchy in France and England: *From the Tenth to the Thirteenth Century* ○ △
TB/1165

HENRI PIRENNE: Early Democracies in the Low Countries: *Urban Society and Political Conflict in the Middle Ages and the Renaissance. Introduction by John M. Mundy*
TB/1110

STEVEN RUNCIMAN: A History of the Crusades. △
Volume I: *The First Crusade and the Foundation of the Kingdom of Jerusalem. Illus.*
TB/1143
Volume II: *The Kingdom of Jerusalem and the Frankish East, 1100-1187. Illus.*
TB/1243
Volume III: *The Kingdom of Acre and the Later Crusades*
TB/1298

FERDINAND SCHEVILL: Siena: *The History of a Medieval Commune. Intro. by William M. Bowsky*
TB/1164

SULPICIUS SEVERUS et al.: The Western Fathers: *Being the Lives of Martin of Tours, Ambrose, Augustine of Hippo, Honoratus of Arles and Germanus of Auxerre.* △ *Edited and trans. by F. O. Hoare*
TB/309

HENRY OSBORN TAYLOR: The Classical Heritage of the Middle Ages. *Foreword and Biblio. by Kenneth M. Setton*
TB/1117

F. VAN DER MEER: Augustine The Bishop: *Church and Society at the Dawn of the Middle Ages* △
TB/304

J. M. WALLACE-HADRILL: The Barbarian West: *The Early Middle Ages, A.D. 400-1000* △
TB/1061

History: Renaissance & Reformation

JACOB BURCKHARDT: The Civilization of the Renaissance in Italy. △ *Intro. by Benjamin Nelson & Charles Trinkaus. Illus.*   Vol. I TB/40; Vol. II TB/41

JOHN CALVIN & JACOPO SADOLETO: A Reformation Debate. *Edited by John C. Olin*
TB/1239

ERNST CASSIRER: The Individual and the Cosmos in Renaissance Philosophy. △ *Translated with an Introduction by Mario Domandi*
TB/1097

FEDERICO CHABOD: Machiavelli and the Renaissance △
TB/1193

EDWARD P. CHEYNEY: The Dawn of a New Era, 1250-1453. * *Illus.*
TB/3002

G. CONSTANT: The Reformation in England: *The English Schism, Henry VIII, 1509-1547* △
TB/314

R. TREVOR DAVIES: The Golden Century of Spain, 1501-1621 ○ △
TB/1194

G. R. ELTON: Reformation Europe, 1517-1559 ** ○ △
TB/1270

DESIDERIUS ERASMUS: Christian Humanism and the Reformation: *Selected Writings. Edited and translated by John C. Olin*
TB/1166

WALLACE K. FERGUSON et al.: Facets of the Renaissance
TB/1098

WALLACE K. FERGUSON et al.: The Renaissance: *Six Essays. Illus.*
TB/1084

JOHN NEVILLE FIGGIS: The Divine Right of Kings. *Introduction by G. R. Elton*
TB/1191

JOHN NEVILLE FIGGIS: Political Thought from Gerson to Grotius: 1414-1625: *Seven Studies. Introduction by Garrett Mattingly*
TB/1032

MYRON P. GILMORE: The World of Humanism, 1453-1517. * *Illus.*
TB/3003

FRANCESCO GUICCIARDINI: Maxims and Reflections of a Renaissance Statesman *(Ricordi). Trans. by Mario Domandi. Intro. by Nicolai Rubinstein*
TB/1160

J. H. HEXTER: More's Utopia: *The Biography of an Idea. New Epilogue by the Author*
TB/1195

HAJO HOLBORN: Ulrich von Hutten and the German Reformation
TB/1238

JOHAN HUIZINGA: Erasmus and the Age of Reformation. △ *Illus.*
TB/19

JOEL HURSTFIELD, Ed.: The Reformation Crisis △
TB/1267

ULRICH VON HUTTEN et al.: On the Eve of the Reformation: *"Letters of Obscure Men." Introduction by Hajo Holborn*
TB/1124

PAUL O. KRISTELLER: Renaissance Thought: *The Classic, Scholastic, and Humanist Strains*
TB/1048

PAUL O. KRISTELLER: Renaissance Thought II: *Papers on Humanism and the Arts*
TB/1163

NICCOLÒ MACHIAVELLI: History of Florence and of the Affairs of Italy: *from the earliest times to the death of Lorenzo the Magnificent.* △ *Introduction by Felix Gilbert*
TB/1027

ALFRED VON MARTIN: Sociology of the Renaissance. *Introduction by Wallace K. Ferguson*
TB/1099

GARRETT MATTINGLY et al.: Renaissance Profiles. △ *Edited by J. H. Plumb*
TB/1162

MILLARD MEISS: Painting in Florence and Siena after the Black Death: *The Arts, Religion and Society in the Mid-Fourteenth Century.* △ *169 illus.*
TB/1148

J. E. NEALE: The Age of Catherine de Medici ○ △ TB/1085

ERWIN PANOFSKY: Studies in Iconology: *Humanistic Themes in the Art of the Renaissance.* △ *180 illustrations*
TB/1077

J. H. PARRY: The Establishment of the European Hegemony: 1415-1715: *Trade and Exploration in the Age of the Renaissance* △
TB/1045

J. H. PLUMB: The Italian Renaissance: *A Concise Survey of Its History and Culture* △
TB/1161

A. F. POLLARD: Henry VIII. ○ △ *Introduction by A. G. Dickens*
TB/1249

A. F. POLLARD: Wolsey. ○ △ *Introduction by A. G. Dickens*
TB/1248

CECIL ROTH: The Jews in the Renaissance. *Illus.* TB/834

A. L. ROWSE: The Expansion of Elizabethan England. ○ △ *Illus.*
TB/1220

GORDON RUPP: Luther's Progress to the Diet of Worms ○ △
TB/120

FERDINAND SCHEVILL: The Medici. *Illus.*
TB/1010

FERDINAND SCHEVILL: Medieval and Renaissance Florence. *Illus.*   Volume I: *Medieval Florence* TB/1090
Volume II: *The Coming of Humanism and the Age of the Medici*
TB/1091

G. M. TREVELYAN: England in the Age of Wycliffe, 1368-1520 ○ △
TB/1112

VESPASIANO: Renaissance Princes, Popes, and Prelates: *The Vespasiano Memoirs: Lives of Illustrious Men of the XVth Century. Intro. by Myron P. Gilmore*
TB/1111

4

Intellectual History & History of Ideas

6

JOHN B. MORRALL: Political Thought in Medieval Times △ TB/1076

JOHN PLAMENATZ: German Marxism and Russian Communism. ° △ New Preface by the Author TB/1189

KARL R. POPPER: The Open Society and Its Enemies △
Vol. I: The Spell of Plato TB/1101
Vol. II: The High Tide of Prophecy: Hegel, Marx and the Aftermath TB/1102

HENRI DE SAINT-SIMON: Social Organization, The Science of Man, and Other Writings. Edited and Translated by Felix Markham TB/1152

JOSEPH A. SCHUMPETER: Capitalism, Socialism and Democracy △ TB/3008

BENJAMIN I. SCHWARTZ: Chinese Communism and the Rise of Mao TB/1308

CHARLES H. SHINN: Mining Camps: A Study in American Frontier Government. ‡ Edited by Rodman W. Paul TB/3062

PETER WOLL, Ed.: Public Administration and Policy: Selected Essays TB/1284

Psychology

ALFRED ADLER: The Individual Psychology of Alfred Adler. △ Edited by Heinz L. and Rowena R. Ansbacher TB/1154

ALFRED ADLER: Problems of Neurosis. Introduction by Heinz L. Ansbacher TB/1145

ANTON T. BOISEN: The Exploration of the Inner World: A Study of Mental Disorder and Religious Experience TB/87

ARTHUR BURTON & ROBERT E. HARRIS, Eds.: Clinical Studies of Personality
Vol. I TB/3075; Vol. II TB/3076

HADLEY CANTRIL: The Invasion from Mars: A Study in the Psychology of Panic ¶ TB/1282

HERBERT FINGARETTE: The Self in Transformation: Psychoanalysis, Philosophy and the Life of the Spirit ¶ TB/1177

SIGMUND FREUD: On Creativity and the Unconscious: Papers on the Psychology of Art, Literature, Love, Religion. § △ Intro. by Benjamin Nelson TB/45

C. JUDSON HERRICK: The Evolution of Human Nature TB/545

WILLIAM JAMES: Psychology: The Briefer Course. Edited with an Intro. by Gordon Allport TB/1034

C. G. JUNG: Psychological Reflections △ TB/2001

C. G. JUNG: Symbols of Transformation: An Analysis of the Prelude to a Case of Schizophrenia. △ Illus.
Vol. I TB/2009; Vol. II TB/2010

C. G. JUNG & C. KERÉNYI: Essays on a Science of Mythology: The Myths of the Divine Child and the Divine Maiden TB/2014

JOHN T. MC NEILL: A History of the Cure of Souls TB/126

KARL MENNINGER: Theory of Psychoanalytic Technique TB/1144

ERICH NEUMANN: Amor and Psyche: The Psychic Development of the Feminine △ TB/2012

ERICH NEUMANN: The Archetypal World of Henry Moore. △ 107 illus. TB/2020

ERICH NEUMANN: The Origins and History of Consciousness △ Vol. I Illus. TB/2007; Vol. II TB/2008

C. P. OBERNDORF: A History of Psychoanalysis in America TB/1147

RALPH BARTON PERRY: The Thought and Character of William James: Briefer Version TB/1156

JEAN PIAGET, BÄRBEL INHELDER, & ALINA SZEMINSKA: The Child's Conception of Geometry ° △ TB/1146

JOHN H. SCHAAR: Escape from Authority: The Perspectives of Erich Fromm TB/1155

MUZAFER SHERIF: The Psychology of Social Norms TB/3072

Sociology

JACQUES BARZUN: Race: A Study in Superstition. Revised Edition TB/1172

BERNARD BERELSON, Ed.: The Behavioral Sciences Today TB/1127

ABRAHAM CAHAN: The Rise of David Levinsky: A documentary novel of social mobility in early twentieth century America. Intro. by John Higham TB/1028

THOMAS C. COCHRAN: The Inner Revolution: Essays on the Social Sciences in History TB/1140

LEWIS A. COSER, Ed.: Political Sociology TB/1293

ALLISON DAVIS & JOHN DOLLARD: Children of Bondage: The Personality Development of Negro Youth in the Urban South ¶ TB/3049

ST. CLAIR DRAKE & HORACE R. CAYTON: Black Metropolis: A Study of Negro Life in a Northern City. △ Revised and Enlarged. Intro. by Everett C. Hughes
Vol. I TB/1086; Vol. II TB/1087

EMILE DURKHEIM et al.: Essays on Sociology and Philosophy: With Analyses of Durkheim's Life and Work. ¶ Edited by Kurt H. Wolff TB/1151

LEON FESTINGER, HENRY W. RIECKEN & STANLEY SCHACHTER: When Prophecy Fails: A Social and Psychological Account of a Modern Group that Predicted the Destruction of the World ¶ TB/1132

ALVIN W. GOULDNER: Wildcat Strike: A Study in Worker-Management Relationships ¶ TB/1176

FRANCIS J. GRUND: Aristocracy in America: Social Class in the Formative Years of the New Nation △ TB/1001

KURT LEWIN: Field Theory in Social Science: Selected Theoretical Papers. ¶ △ Edited with a Foreword by Dorwin Cartwright TB/1135

R. M. MAC IVER: Social Causation TB/1153

ROBERT K. MERTON, LEONARD BROOM, LEONARD S. COTTRELL, JR., Editors: Sociology Today: Problems and Prospects ¶ . Vol. I TB/1173; Vol. II TB/1174

ROBERTO MICHELS: First Lectures in Political Sociology. Edited by Alfred de Grazia ¶ ° TB/1224

BARRINGTON MOORE, JR.: Political Power and Social Theory: Seven Studies ¶ TB/1221

BARRINGTON MOORE, JR.: Soviet Politics—The Dilemma of Power: The Role of Ideas in Social Change ¶ TB/1222

TALCOTT PARSONS & EDWARD A. SHILS, Editors: Toward a General Theory of Action: Theoretical Foundations for the Social Sciences TB/1083

JOHN H. ROHRER & MUNRO S. EDMONDSON, Eds.: The Eighth Generation Grows Up: Cultures and Personalities of New Orleans Negroes ¶ TB/3050

ARNOLD ROSE: The Negro in America: The Condensed Version of Gunnar Myrdal's An American Dilemma TB/3048

KURT SAMUELSSON: Religion and Economic Action: A Critique of Max Weber's The Protestant Ethic and the Spirit of Capitalism. ¶ ° Trans. by E. G. French. Ed. with Intro. by D. C. Coleman TB/1131

PHILIP SELZNICK: TVA and the Grass Roots: A Study in the Sociology of Formal Organization TB/1230

GEORG SIMMEL et al.: Essays on Sociology, Philosophy, and Aesthetics. ¶ Edited by Kurt H. Wolff TB/1234

HERBERT SIMON: The Shape of Automation: For Men and Management △ TB/1245

PITIRIM A. SOROKIN: Contemporary Sociological Theories. Through the First Quarter of the 20th Century TB/3046

MAURICE R. STEIN: The Eclipse of Community: An Interpretation of American Studies TB/1128

FERDINAND TÖNNIES: Community and Society: Gemeinschaft und Gesellschaft. Translated and edited by Charles P. Loomis TB/1116

W. LLOYD WARNER & Associates: Democracy in Jonesville: A Study in Quality and Inequality TB/1129

W. LLOYD WARNER: Social Class in America: The Evaluation of Status TB/1013

RELIGION

Ancient & Classical

J. H. BREASTED: Development of Religion and Thought in Ancient Egypt. *Intro. by John A. Wilson* TB/57

HENRI FRANKFORT: Ancient Egyptian Religion: *An Interpretation* TB/77

G. RACHEL LEVY: Religious Conceptions of the Stone Age and their Influence upon European Thought. △ *Illus. Introduction by Henri Frankfort* TB/106

MARTIN P. NILSSON: Greek Folk Religion. *Foreword by Arthur Darby Nock* TB/78

ALEXANDRE PIANKOFF: The Shrines of Tut-Ankh-Amon. △ *Edited by N. Rambova. 117 illus.* TB/2011

ERWIN ROHDE: Psyche: *The Cult of Souls and Belief in Immortality Among the Greeks.* △ *Intro. by W. K. C. Guthrie* Vol. I TB/140; Vol. II TB/141

H. J. ROSE: Religion in Greece and Rome △ TB/55

Biblical Thought & Literature

W. F. ALBRIGHT: The Biblical Period from Abraham to Ezra TB/102

C. K. BARRETT, Ed.: The New Testament Background: *Selected Documents* △ TB/86

C. H. DODD: The Authority of the Bible △ TB/43

M. S. ENSLIN: Christian Beginnings △ TB/5

M. S. ENSLIN: The Literature of the Christian Movement △ TB/6

JOHN GRAY: Archaeology and the Old Testament World. △ *Illus.* TB/127

JAMES MUILENBURG: The Way of Israel: *Biblical Faith and Ethics* △ TB/133

H. H. ROWLEY: The Growth of the Old Testament △ TB/107

GEORGE ADAM SMITH: The Historical Geography of the Holy Land. △ *Revised and reset* TB/138

D. WINTON THOMAS, Ed.: Documents from Old Testament Times △ TB/85

WALTHER ZIMMERLI: The Law and the Prophets: *A Study of the Meaning of the Old Testament* △ TB/144

The Judaic Tradition

LEO BAECK: Judaism and Christianity. *Trans. with Intro. by Walter Kaufmann* TB/823

SALO W. BARON: Modern Nationalism and Religion JP/18

MARTIN BUBER: Eclipse of God: *Studies in the Relation Between Religion and Philosophy* △ TB/12

MARTIN BUBER: For the Sake of Heaven TB/801

MARTIN BUBER: Hasidism and Modern Man. △ *Ed. and Trans. by Maurice Friedman* TB/839

MARTIN BUBER: The Knowledge of Man. △ *Edited with an Introduction by Maurice Friedman. Translated by Maurice Friedman and Ronald Gregor Smith* TB/135

MARTIN BUBER: Moses: *The Revelation and the Covenant* △ TB/837

MARTIN BUBER: The Origin and Meaning of Hasidism △ TB/835

MARTIN BUBER: Pointing the Way. △ *Introduction by Maurice S. Friedman* TB/103

MARTIN BUBER: The Prophetic Faith TB/73

MARTIN BUBER: Two Types of Faith: *the interpenetration of Judaism and Christianity* ○ △ TB/75

ERNST LUDWIG EHRLICH: A Concise History of Israel: *From the Earliest Times to the Destruction of the Temple in A.D. 70* ○ △ TB/128

MAURICE S. FRIEDMAN: Martin Buber: *The Life of Dialogue* △ TB/64

GENESIS: *The NJV Translation* TB/836

SOLOMON GRAYZEL: A History of the Contemporary Jews TB/816

WILL HERBERG: Judaism and Modern Man TB/810

ARTHUR HERTZBERG: The Zionist Idea TB/817

ABRAHAM J. HESCHEL: God in Search of Man: *A Philosophy of Judaism* TB/807

ISAAC HUSIK: A History of Medieval Jewish Philosophy TB/803

FLAVIUS JOSEPHUS: The Great Roman-Jewish War, *with The Life of Josephus. Introduction by William R. Farmer* TB/74

JACOB R. MARCUS: The Jew in the Medieval World TB/814

MAX L. MARGOLIS & ALEXANDER MARX: A History of the Jewish People TB/806

T. J. MEEK: Hebrew Origins TB/69

JAMES PARKES: The Conflict of the Church and the Synagogue: *The Jews and Early Christianity* JP/21

PHILO, SAADYA GAON, & JEHUDA HALEVI: Three Jewish Philosophers. *Ed. by Hans Lewey, Alexander Altmann, & Isaak Heinemann* TB/813

CECIL ROTH: A History of the Marranos TB/812

CECIL ROTH: The Jews in the Renaissance. *Illus.* TB/834

HERMAN L. STRACK: Introduction to the Talmud and Midrash TB/808

JOSHUA TRACHTENBERG: The Devil and the Jews: *The Medieval Conception of the Jew and its Relation to Modern Anti-Semitism* TB/822

Christianity: General

ROLAND H. BAINTON: Christendom: *A Short History of Christianity and its Impact on Western Civilization.* △ *Illus.* Vol. I TB/131; Vol. II TB/132

Christianity: Origins & Early Development

AUGUSTINE: An Augustine Synthesis. △ *Edited by Erich Przywara* TB/335

ADOLF DEISSMANN: Paul: *A Study in Social and Religious History* TB/15

EDWARD GIBBON: The Triumph of Christendom in the Roman Empire *(Chaps. XV-XX of "Decline and Fall," J. B. Bury edition).* § △ *Illus.* TB/46

MAURICE GOGUEL: Jesus and the Origins of Christianity. ○ △ *Introduction by C. Leslie Mitton* Volume I: *Prolegomena to the Life of Jesus* TB/65 Volume II: *The Life of Jesus* TB/66

EDGAR J. GOODSPEED: A Life of Jesus TB/1

ROBERT M. GRANT: Gnosticism and Early Christianity. △ *Revised Edition* TB/136

ADOLF HARNACK: The Mission and Expansion of Christianity in the First Three Centuries. *Introduction by Jaroslav Pelikan* TB/92

R. K. HARRISON: The Dead Sea Scrolls : *An Introduction* ○ △ TB/84

EDWIN HATCH: The Influence of Greek Ideas on Christianity. § △ *Introduction and Bibliography by Frederick C. Grant* TB/18

ARTHUR DARBY NOCK: Early Gentile Christianity and Its Hellenistic Background TB/111

ARTHUR DARBY NOCK: St. Paul ○ △ TB/104

ORIGEN: On First Principles. △ *Edited by G. W. Butterworth. Introduction by Henri de Lubac* TB/311

JAMES PARKES: The Conflict of the Church and the Synagogue: *The Jews and Early Christianity* JP/21

SULPICIUS SEVERUS et al.: The Western Fathers: *Being the Lives of Martin of Tours, Ambrose, Augustine of Hippo, Honoratus of Arles and Germanus of Auxerre.* △ *Edited and translated by F. R. Hoare* TB/309

F. VAN DER MEER: Augustine the Bishop: *Church and Society at the Dawn of the Middle Ages* △ TB/304

JOHANNES WEISS: Earliest Christianity: *A History of the Period A.D. 30-150. Introduction and Bibliography by Frederick C. Grant* Volume I TB/53 Volume II TB/54

Christianity: The Middle Ages and The Reformation

ANSELM OF CANTERBURY: Truth, Freedom and Evil: *Three Philosophical Dialogues. Ed., trans., and Intro. by Jasper Hopkins & Herbert Richardson* TB/317

11